# All the World in a Blade of Quack

## RECLAIMING A GARDEN
## GROWING A GARDENER

Coleen Johnston

NORTH STAR PRESS OF ST. CLOUD, INC.
St. Cloud, Minnesota

To the late Bette Johnston Pickard
for inspiring my love of flower gardening,
birds,
and nature's wonders

ISBN 978-0-87839-581-1

First Edition: June 2012

Printed in the United States of America

Published by
North Star Press of St. Cloud, Inc.
P.O. Box 451
St. Cloud, Minnesota 56302

www.northstarpress.com

# Table of Contents

# 1

# Live Things

*I came into the world
one day when I stepped
outside my door*

On hands and knees, I finished weeding a three-foot clump of peonies orbited by a galaxy of shiny pink buds and stretched to straighten out my back. I looked up to see how many clumps were left to go. Twenty-one. Oh, dear. At the same moment, on the other side of the clump, a wild turkey straightened his neck up to see what had interrupted his lunch.

Our eyes met. His bulged, and I was close enough that I could see he didn't have any lashes. He froze. I screamed. His shriveled, tomato-red wattle pulsed and looked like something decency would dictate he keep on the inside of his feathers. He opened his beak (a gasp?), then snapped it shut.

My arms shot up, waving in wild frenzy. He didn't move. But his eyes started swelling like two red balloons being slowly inflated.

1

"Aaaaaaaaah!!!"

Not a feather moved on the big, black body.

Great, a deaf turkey.

I froze, too. Could I outrun a turkey?

Maybe it was my stillness that finally did the trick. He turned, soundlessly, creeping away with long strides and bobbing neck, his wattle swinging side to side and his gray beard a silent ghost leading the way, as if by going quietly he might erase his appearance. His black tail almost touched the ground—quite beautiful, really, once it was in retreat.

My heart pounded as I returned to my futile attempt to rid the peonies of two decades of weeds—mostly quack grass. On my knees, my elbows resting on the cool soil, I continued to wrap each blade of quack around my index finger and pull. Most of them broke off instead of sliding all the way out, leaving behind bazillions of quack roots, which would immediately begin to grow back, a fact I knew but felt powerless to change—short of digging up the whole garden.

The peony clumps stood shoulder to shoulder in a row that ran from one end of the garden to the other, over a hundred feet, and had not been divided in at least twenty years. They were just ready to burst into bloom. I wanted them to look their best for the big show, so I kept on working.

An hour later, almost certain the turkey would not return, my hands quit shaking.

Some people garden because they like to have fresh vegetables to eat. Some want organic. Some garden for the scents of lavender and rose. Some want to add color to their lives. Some garden because they aren't able to play football, or don't believe in gambling with cards. Some are scientists who like to experiment, even though they never got beyond ninth-grade biology. Some have gardening born into them. Some, like me, feel an obligation to restore what has been lost and to re-cycle what is left—no matter what the cost.

The turkey cost me a few heartbeats. As one who can imagine a Venus fly trap biting off her foot or a sheet of moss smothering her, I was not the ideal candidate for the task of reclaiming a garden overgrown with waist-high weeds. At first, just looking at the wild tangle inspired a fear that made the thought of stepping into a place where snakes might slither across my feet almost too much to bear. Many kids can't wait to pick up any injured or disabled creature they find, but I grew up with a fear of live things, albeit most of them were animal rather than vegetable. Still, even as an adult, I can imagine crawly creatures everywhere, especially in weeds.

Growing up on a farm means that plants and animals are your life. Even though I only lived there until I was nine, the farm gave me a healthy respect for stinging nettles, yellow rocket, and pigweed, as well as for getting kicked, bitten, and pooped on. (Getting rabies also seemed like something imperative to avoid.) The farm taught me to be careful of getting my clothes dirty and provided my first sights of death, too. Many farm kids I knew had learned to accept the sight of dead things—the piglets born dead or the sick cow that doesn't make it—as sad but routine parts of the business of farming. I just couldn't look at them at all.

I grew up scared of living things because they squirmed and didn't talk, and dead things because they were, well, dead. I despaired of touching dead plants for fear of getting green, oogy stuff on my hands. Even sick plants seemed way beyond the scope of my small world. Early on I developed an attachment to inanimate objects, which I clung to fiercely, knowing I was surely destined to end up with a house that looked like the backroom of a furniture store but satisfied that none of it squirmed, pooped, or died.

People who do not like either dead things or live things should never move to the country, the kingdom of quack grass, where the sight of dead raccoons on the road and slugs inching up the hostas are everyday occurrences. They should never have gardens where earwigs and beetles, and the occasional snake, coexist with toads and birds and mice that scurry under one's feet from their nests in the Siberian irises. Most of all, they should never get face to face with the earth, because once they start, they will never be the same.

Like many whose dream it is to return to their roots, our family moved to the country after twenty-plus years of urban, but mostly small-town, life. Gardening in town, where I could run out and stand in the middle of the street until a rabbit ate his way out of the lettuce, did not prepare me for all of the living things I would encounter in a woodland setting. All of us think that we know a lot about nature—

we've been to parks and gardens and museums, or studied biology and botany—but experiences and study only scratch the surface of the world outside our door.

I had seen wild turkeys grazing in farm fields for years, but the up-close and personal look at the one who wanted to share my peonies told me that the world wasn't something I could hold at arm's length, and neither could the turkey. After all, he was obviously another creature who didn't care for live things. Then again, maybe he thought I was a dead thing (a thought that makes me reconsider my self-worth).

In any case, once he was safely away in the cover of the woods, only about twenty feet from the garden's edge, I was able to get on with my work in the peonies. I could hear my long-departed parents' voices in my ear: "You don't need to be afraid of a deer [or porcupine or snake/fish/worm—you name it] because it's a lot more afraid of you than you are of it." That advice had served me well when they were around to protect me, but here I was, in a garden in the country and not another person within a half-mile, almost completely surrounded by woodland, and I had to wonder if animals were truly all that afraid of people. Even if they were, there was still the chance that I could die of fright from the sight of one alone.

For the next few moments after the turkey episode, I looked up over the peony plants every few seconds, expecting the worst. But, finally, all seemed safe. Had I conquered? Or had a truce been declared? I chose to think of our existence as a truce. I would stay on my side of the woods and he on his.

One thing was clear: I had inspired fear in another living being to which I meant no harm. Didn't the turkey realize that he scared me more than I scared him? If he did, he still decided that sneaking off was his best option. It is good to trust your instincts, I decided—mine to shriek and his to sneak away. And I wished that I could erase the mistakes I'd made, just as he tried to erase his ill-timed appearance.

We were not so different, this turkey and I. He didn't realize the vibes I got when he opened his beak and then clamped it shut. Or maybe he did. He communicated. I communicated. The very thought gave a whole new meaning to the term "talking turkey."

I knew I was fitting into my new place when I realized that I was communicating with non-human, live things on some level, even if it was still a panic level, but it didn't start out that way. It all started with the green monster, and I don't mean the Fenway Park wall of ivy. I mean the untamed beast with whom I did not intend to call a truce: Quack.

Did you ever wonder how to get the ants off peonies before you bring them in the house? One good way is to pick the buds just before they open, when they are like big marshmallows, because the ants will still be on the outside and can be easily brushed off (or dip the buds in water, then shake off). Once in the house, they will open ant-free. Peony buds can also be cut and held in the refrigerator for up to a month (even longer, if you're lucky)—so if you want to have fresh peonies at a wedding in August, pick the buds in June, put them in a plastic bag in the refrigerator with the stem ends exposed, and then cut an inch or so off the ends when ready for use. They may take up to forty-eight hours to open, so you'll need to experiment.

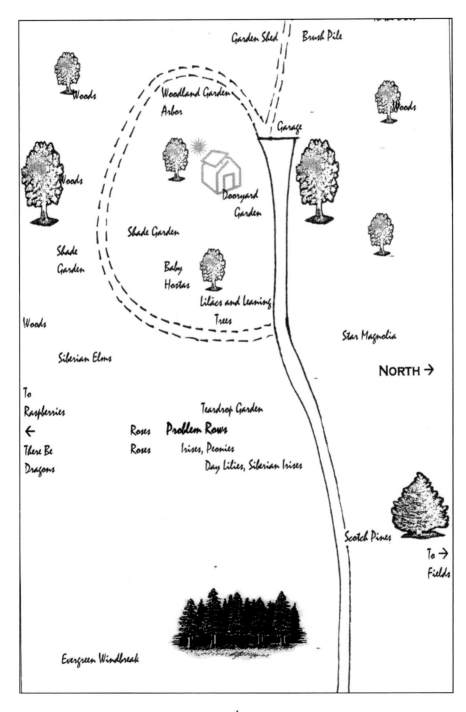

# 2

# Bigger Than I Thought

Most people buying property in the country ask to see the property lines before they sign the papers so that they know where their land ends and their neighbor's begins. The seller's realtor, an impeccably groomed woman in a professional looking gray suit, is less than eager to trek through woods and fields trying to find stakes. She says that the neighbors could probably give us better information than she can. We leave it at that. We inspect every mitered corner and grout joint in the house, but we blow off the property's boundaries.

When it comes to actually living on the property, we realize that we need to find out how to tell if we are on our own side of the line or over it so that we don't begin our sojourn there on the wrong side of everybody. With my husband away at a seminar, daughter off at college, and son busy with high school, I come to our new home alone that first day, determined to get us off on the right foot. The property has a long, paved driveway that meanders through a park-like lawn bordered with massive evergreens. The handyman who took care of the place for the previous owners has it all looking very sharp.

As I drive up, fresh from signing papers at the bank, I look at the four rows of two-foot high quack grass making an S-curve along the west side of the lawn. Each row is about 100 feet long. Although the rest of the lawn is freshly cut, green, and beautiful, these four rows of weeds are all I can see. I already know that irises and peonies lurk inside the mess. I know I am going to have to do something about it, but at first I don't know what. There is a lot more of it than there is of me. I stop the car in the middle of the driveway and give the long rows a hard look: I'm going to get rid of it all, I decide. I know it was quite beautiful once, and could be again, but I have my limits.

I scan beyond the rows of ragged quack for the rosebushes at the top of the gradual slope, where the realtor told us there once was a large garden. The roses, of course, are also afloat in a sea of weeds. I promise myself I will take care of the roses because I can see they are mostly old-fashioned shrub varieties and will not require much of my time. I know there is also a hosta garden up by the house and am sure I can manage that. I can keep it all looking nice, if I don't have too much of it and if I stick to "easy-care" plants.

The new property, our dream home, has been vacant for a year and needs considerable work. As an avid do-it-herselfer, I look forward to it but, even so, I want to keep it all manageable. Whatever that means.

Before I can unlock the door to the new house, I see our neighbor walking up the driveway. He has agreed to meet me at one o'clock so that we can walk the property lines, and he is right on time. Our brown-and-white springer spaniel, Brule, bounces out of the car to go with us, as excited about the new place as I am. She threads her way, nose to the ground, through the long grass, always a few yards ahead of us. Hay stubble crunches under my feet as I cross the hay field we now own.

The neighbor has been renting the ten acres for many years and will now also rent from us. Our property, I find, has only one length of fence running from west to east, most of it lost under decades of elderberry brush and wild elms and poplars that, by the look of them, can only be cleaned up by several days with a Bobcat. My neighbor says that the lack of fences isn't bothering him, so if it doesn't bother us we can just leave everything as is. It isn't bothering us, but should it? I hear Frost's line "good fences make good neighbors" somewhere in the back of my head, but I push it away. It looks as though we are going to be blessed with good neighbors here just as we were at our old house.

After the new neighbor shows me the large post on the northwest corner—the one property line marker he knows for sure—he suggests we might be able to find the southwest marker too, although he is less certain of the boundaries of our fifteen acres of woods, which is the part where the house sits.

I follow his long strides due south from the known northwest marker, my white Nikes no match for his tall brown boots, especially once we leave the relatively smooth hay ground for the woods, where a deep ravine is dotted with thorny gooseberry brush and various kinds of stickers and burrs. He avoids the steepest path yet keeps on course, and after we pass the buildings and walk farther up another hill and back down, he finds it: a simple iron fence post staked all alone amid pillars of tree trunks.

Above us, the sun shimmers through the gold, orange, and russet leaves of oaks, basswood, and black cherry trees, along with others that I can't identify.

I don't know why I am so surprised to find the post with its florescent pink tag in the middle of the forest, but I am. I have never believed it possible to mark boundaries in woodlands, I suppose, because it doesn't seem feasible to try to fence around hundreds of trees. Nevertheless, here is a rusted brown post, quietly performing its duty.

Brule is already sniffing the base of the post, probably picking up on some ancient scent, but I would have missed it completely had it not been for the pink tag. The stake, which has been in place at least since the house was built on our property, has remained in place because it has no natural predators. It is in all of the neighbors' best interests to just leave it alone, and there are no animals large enough to knock it down. It is, no doubt, set so deeply in the earth that it will not just fall over (the way it could have if I had set it), and so it is secure. People know the stake is there, but they don't lie awake at night worrying about it, the way I had the night I realized that if we could not find the stake we might have to pay to have the property surveyed.

Thanks to our neighbor, I now know, more or less, the outer boundaries of the property. The sense of its size comes as quite an education: I had always heard farms referred to in terms of acreage, but had never really known how much twenty-five acres actually looked like. Now I know. It's bigger than I thought. I can't see all the way across it (although I could if it were all open land), and I get out of breath just from walking across it.

As I watch the neighbor start for home, walking across the hay field with its modest fence, I wonder about the whole "good fences" and "good neighbors" thing. The unfenced sides remind me of what people with invisible dog fences have told me: the invisible fence is good for keeping one's own dog in but worthless for keeping other dogs out. Obviously there is nothing here that needs to be kept out, or in. Crops and woodlands cooperate to define their own boundaries. A sensible arrangement, I decide.

Our property boundaries seem to be based on trust: trust that we will not cut our neighbors' trees down and that they will not cut ours. Trust that our renters will plow and plant only our ten acres and not any of the other neighbors', whose furrows lie exactly parallel and only a tractor tire's width away. Trust that other people will not decide to drive in and scatter thistle seed, or worse.

Fences take up space, and so our neighbor would not be able to produce as much if the whole field were fenced in. Fences are expensive to build and take time to maintain—a job that is now ours and something I haven't considered in the fever of having the chance to own a place in the country. I try to get a grip on the fact that the acres have been farmed for a long time just as they are, mostly fenceless. Still, my childhood teachings as to what comprised a "good" farm—one with strong, neat fences—make me wonder if we will be seen as terribly deficient landowners if we don't maintain at least the one fence we share with this neighbor.

"Making fence," as it is called, is a hard job. I think of the stone fences in New England, born of the necessity of getting rocks out of the field, and my back hurts. Still, something from my love of collecting rocks at Lake Superior when I was a kid, and of having helped my uncle Bob build a stone fireplace when I was ten years old makes me think I might actually have enjoyed stacking those granite puzzles, had my ancestors stayed in Maine. But they hadn't.

Fence making in the Midwest has traditionally been a post-and-wire operation. Fences near roadways will be judged and discussed by other farmers, and so these must be made as neatly as possible, using new posts, either wood or metal. Away from those critical eyes, fences can be made of any material at hand: old railroad ties, dead trees, or maybe beams from the shed that fell down under last winter's snow load.

Fence making as such is not a glorious pursuit. Any farmer would rather be tilling and sowing than making fence, or even "fixing fence"—repairing the places where cattle broke through or vandals cut through or trees fell through. Fences aren't forever. They aren't perfect. Yet, in light of "good fences make good neighbors," they do seem desirable and maybe even necessary.

Essayist and poet Wendell Berry says that "the question of human limits . . . finally rests upon our attitude toward our biological existence, the life of the body in this world." It is my body I am thinking about this first day. Can my body physically fix houses and fences and weeds without end? Can my body find time to do all these things and more? I consider these questions and find myself coming up short in the qualifications department: no experience, no muscles toned from exercise and weight lifting, no extra time. Up until I saw the lack of fences, I hadn't considered all that we are buying into here. Now I feel panic rising like a rocket.

What does it mean, this need to set limits? Maybe it's fear of failure. After all, we guard against failure by defining what we can and can't do, and then go beyond those things only at great risk to our psyches should we fail. No one wants to fail. Thus we are a limit-encouraging society. We encourage limits in the workplace so as not to get into messy entanglements with people (probably a good idea), limits where job encroaches on home life (easier prescribed than adhered to), limits on spending (to keep society out of debt—and this isn't working all that well), and limits for our pets (Brule does not seem to believe that limits apply to her).

I walk back to the house, past the long rows of quack. Again. My worry about fences now commingles with the problem of the quack in the irises. Only later do I open up a book of Frost's poems and read the rest of "Mending Wall."

> Before I built a wall I'd ask to know
> what I was walling in or walling out,
> and to whom I was like to give offense.
> Something there is that doesn't love a wall
> that wants it down.

Aha! Frost would rise up and pen an Op-Ed for the *New York Times* if he knew he were being remembered for "good fences make good neighbors," because clearly he meant the opposite. Fortunately, I forget my fear of fencelessness (of being defenceless?) as soon as I get back in the house and look out the east window. There is Brule, just below the window, chewing on quack grass at the edge of the hosta garden. Quack, I am sure, will take over the whole twenty-five acres if I am not careful.

Beyond Brule lie the long rows of quack. Why have the previous owners left those right out there for everyone to see? Surely the neighbors judge this every bit as much as they do a derelict fence. I look around at all that needs to be done inside the house, and I fear I can never restore the gardens—unless I stage a coup against the kingdom of quack.

Did you ever wonder how big an acre really is? Imagine three-fourths of a football field and you'll have it. Haven't been to a football field lately? Try thinking of 43,560 square feet instead. It sounds huge, but then, think of a square mile, which contains 640 square acres. Doesn't sound bad at all now, right?

# 3

# A Thing Wished For

I smell the rich compost of newly fallen leaves and the wine of over-ripe raspberries as I walk back to the house after my trek with our neighbor. It is early afternoon on the fifteenth of October, one of those truly golden days when most of the leaves have fallen and nothing separates me from the sun. It is no longer the kind of sun that will give a sunburn and so I soak it up—in Minnesota everyone tries to bank sunshine whenever they can, as if they can withdraw it in January and bring the temp from twenty below all the way up to ten below or even something as exotic as zero.

After I grab the keys out of the car, I head toward the garage service door, acorns plunking out a processional on the pavement. The acorns barely land before squirrels spirit them away. All is beautiful, calm and peaceful. A perfect beginning.

The key ring the real estate agent gave me seems to weigh five pounds and I wonder if I will ever figure out what key goes to what lock. I flick through keys big and little, nickel and brass, round- and square-topped, trying several before I come to the one that opens the door. When the lock finally clicks, Brule runs ahead of me into the dark garage, which is every bit as dim as the driveway is bright. I step inside, groping for the light switch. The garage is cool, damp and completely empty, something that will change drastically as we start moving in. We are just up the steps and into the kitchen when I hear a woodpecker outside, drilling away at the cedar siding. It's clear that woodpeckers see the house as just another big tree. Obviously, not everybody needs a key.

This first day at the new house I count myself lucky to have two weeks to work on the house before moving in. The twenty-year-old house is in beautiful condition, but we want to redecorate and make it our own. If we are to paint, tile, carpet, renovate and still move in by October 31, we will have to scurry. Everything has to happen in sequence. Like General George S. Patton, I must coordinate and carry out a mission against insurmountable odds—meeting all of my deadlines. Still, I don't start working right away. Instead, I walk into the empty living room and look out the bay window at a small, leafless patch of woods, then beyond it to those long rows of quacked-in irises and peonies. I look again at the pigweed and deadwood in the roses, at the weed patch that can only be identified as a shade garden because two giant variegated hostas are fighting their way to the top of a mass of plants too short to be shrubs and not woody enough to be trees. Can this all be weeds? I can't tell. But I do know that the only semblance of control in the garden is the edge cut by the mower. There is a message in that.

I check the south window hoping to see a deer or fox, even though I know mid-afternoon is not the time to see them. On this first day in this new place, however, anything seems possible. The place feels so perfect I almost believe a thing wished for might well translate into a thing realized, but my wish for a fox or a deer doesn't come true. Still, when the friend who is going to help me paint and wallpaper arrives a few minutes later and we walk out onto the deck so that she can look around, she turns her face to the sun, oblivious of her tendency to freckle. "It just doesn't get any better than this," she says. "I've never wanted to live in the country, but I would love to live *here*."

Obviously she has not seen those four long rows of quack. Or the thistles. Or the raspberry patch without end. But as for the house, the woods and the weather, on this day all seems golden.

It's not until we are moved in and the old house closed on that I take time to walk through the gardens when Brule and I come back from getting the mail. She slaloms through the quack rows and springs over small rose bushes, causing a shower of brown-edged pink petals on the lawn. It is October 30 and everything but the roses have turned a dull khaki. The sun warms my face as I hurry past the quack and roses, clutching an armload of mail, mostly catalogues intended for the previous owner. Slowing down a bit, I walk through the front dooryard garden on the path at the bottom of the limestone retaining wall that tips out at the top and in at the bottom, just the opposite of the way a good retaining wall should. Even so, the stones in the wall and the path will make beautiful features for showing off whatever plants I decide to install, and I know this is a garden I want to restore.

Above the wall, burgundy and bronze mums are bowing their spent heads amid the sea of unknown weeds that don't seem to be dying back like everything else. I see a couple of small rose bushes valiantly trying to maintain their status. Dandelions, ferns, and wild geraniums are having their way with the spaces between the paving stones. It looks as though chickweed eradication will be the challenge here, instead of quack. What a wonderful (I think?) surprise.

Next to the path, I have hastily planted, of all things, irises I brought from the old house. That's right, more irises. Though I know they might not survive the trip, I take a chance because they aren't just any irises. They are irises given to me by a wonderful friend near the end of her gardening days. She wanted me to have them. I couldn't abandon them at the old house. As I check them for signs of life and see that the spears bear only a little green, I sense I will never care for them as my friend had, that I will never be able to care for all of these gardens as did the previous owner, also a friend, who was a master gardener and who had the benefit of hired help, which I will not. I am doomed to fail unless I downsize considerably.

I check off the dooryard garden in my mind as a manageable priority and walk around the house to where I have seen the two big hostas. Here a jungle of unknown weeds along the edge of the woods curves gracefully away from the house under the only birch tree on the property. I will have to do something about this garden. Since I don't know what that might be, I walk on and discover gardens I haven't known *were* gardens along the edge of the woods on the south side of the house. Now that the sumac, elderberries, and other underbrush have lost their leaves, it is possible to see the rose bushes there. Where does the woods end and the garden begin? It all seems to be mixed together.

After a day or two, I can't stand wondering what is in all of these gardens any longer: I need to get out there and do something, or at least make some decisions. The wind is cold and the day gloomy, not at all the kind of day one envisions as a gardening day, but I pull on a vest over a heavy hooded sweatshirt and head directly for the four rows of quack. Maybe I've misjudged it, I tell myself. Maybe I've assumed that cleaning it up was an impossible task even though one lesson I continue to try to teach myself is "never assume." I take off my stretchy knit gloves, bend over and grab a handful of coarse quack, trying not to mix in any of the rapidly browning iris leaves in its midst. Not only can I not pull the wad of quack up by the roots, I really can't pull it up at all—I can only break it off here and there and come close to falling on my fanny in the doing.

The soil is dry and hard, yet quack roots tough as white nylon shipping twine push their way through. My assumption is right: I will never be able to successfully de-quack the irises. I move on to the next row where I remember having seen some peonies, plants I've had more experience with. Sure enough, their yellowed foliage is still there, having sagged under an early frost. Every square inch of ground not filled by peony stems is filled with—what else?—quack. The cold is simultaneously turning my hands a fiery red and a blotchy white. I paw my way into row three. This turns out not to be more irises but instead clumps of daylilies that erupt in small mountains from the quack-carpeted ground below. Their withered leaves extend in all directions like skinny ecru octopi. The last row appears to be just quack. There is no sign of any perennial or annual I can see. Why hasn't it been mowed down long before this? Just a mistake, I assume.

Between each of these rows is a three-foot space of lawn grass, in this case mostly quack, which I see immediately as the most invasive, terrible curse that can befall a garden. Grass and gardens do not mix. At places in the daylily row, some of the grass looks as though it might be ornamental. Planted on purpose. Costly and exotic. I don't care. I make a mental note that, when and if I ever get rid of the quack, all the other grasses are going, too—even the ornamentals. I will not give one more kind of grass a chance to ruin things. I don't even want to know what these grasses are or what my friend might have paid for them. I do not want any. More. Grass.

I pull my gloves back on and give up. In the spring, after rain has softened the ground, I will move a few of the irises and daylilies into a small bed somewhere and call it good. I will save a clump of peonies or two—they can hold their own in the middle of a lawn, or at least my grandmother's always had. The rest will have to go. There is no way to reclaim these rows of flowers without hours—maybe even days or weeks—of back-breaking work. I will not feel like such a terrible person, I tell myself, if I save at least some of them. This thought eases the burning that has begun in the pit of my stomach since I realized there are twenty-five acres and there is only one me.

My hands are dirty, the knees of my blue jeans are grass stained, and I have managed to cut myself on a piece of quack grass, the only green thing among all of the gold of late autumn. I think back to the agreement I made with my husband before we moved in: No fussy gardens, no gardens that require anything more than a once-a-year fertilizing and maybe a new layer of mulch. I will not be chained to a garden. I don't even know that much about gardens. For the time being there is only one thing to do: get out the mower and mow the grass down, plants and all, before winter. It will at least look better that way. I make a mental note to raise the blade over the daylily row.

Even with my gloves on, my hands are cold. I take one last look toward the quack rows on the east lawn. To call them a garden at this point seems too generous, but clearly they were a garden once—or part of one whose size defies my meager imagination. Sometimes lack of imagination is a wonderful gift in that it saves us from getting ahead of ourselves. Imagination that grows in proportion to possibilities grows like, well, a weed once we begin gardening. But I didn't know that then. I only knew that I was beginning to believe in the truth of the old adage: Be careful what you wish for because you might get it.

Did you ever wonder why people started mowing and maintaining lawns? Once lawns were only for the wealthy who could afford to take agricultural land out of production and plant grass instead. The immense, sweeping greens begged for use, and so lawn games became popular and soon everyone wanted a lawn. Still, lawns were not practical for anyone who couldn't afford a regiment of gardeners to trim the grass with scythes until around 1870 when Edwin Budding (great name, eh?) an engineer at a British textile mill, invented the first rotary mower. By 1885, U.S. factories were selling 50,000 mowers every year. Are lawns really easier to maintain than flower gardens? Better for the environment? Prettier? Maybe one day lawns will again be rare—not because of wealth, but because of changing tastes and/or environmental impact issues.

# 4

# When the Time Is Right

We often picture lawn mowing as something done by young shirtless men in the heat of summer, usually with a sweat band riding low over their eyes. We picture it ending with a cold beer or lemonade and the satisfaction of a job well done, maybe even with a few dollars in the pocket. In Minnesota, lawn mowing normally begins in late April, with considerable eagerness, and ends in late October, with considerable relief. By the last mowing, one most often needs a parka and gloves. My first chance to mow the new lawn comes in November, just ahead of the first snow.

We brought our ancient John Deere mower with us from the old house, but had also purchased the larger, wider-swath mower used by the previous owners. Today, at fifty-five degrees, the old mower will not start. I turn the key on the newer model and smile as it blasts into action with a puff of black smoke. Hydrostatic where the old one was manual, this new green machine hits reverse quickly and sends me out of the shed with a hysterical laugh. I lurch into a forward gear without hitting a tree, then practice raising and lowering the deck all the way down the hill toward the rows of quack so that I will be ready to save the daylilies when I get to them.

The lever used for raising the mowing mechanism is obviously intended for use only by men with considerably more muscle mass than I have: it requires me to use both hands to get the job done, but I manage. I also manage not to mow down any known garden plants as I speed toward the lawn below the woods, not yet knowing how to slow the tractor down.

I slam down the brake just at the top of the row of irises and stop in time to find the lever that makes the tractor speed up (rabbit icon) and slow down (turtle icon). What luck! I begin turtle-pacing my way along the row of irises. They cut with no problem. Ditto the peonies. On the daylily row I manage, even with the deck raised, to shear off the tops of every little mound, exposing golden carrot-like roots. The mower makes gravelly, groaning sounds. I make a mental note not to tell my husband about this.

Rabbit-speeding over row four, the tractor decimates the grass without incident. Again I wonder what anyone was saving it for, but at my current rapid speed, and fear of not being able to stop, I do not wonder about it for long.

I complete the first mowing with no sweat, no dollars, and no lemonade, but with the strong sense of a job well done. I drive the little green tractor down the driveway at a speedy clip, hoping to get the long view of my handiwork. The lawn, without the offending rows of quack, now serves as the proper foreground for the woods, and for the house nestled into them as if a robin had built it there.

I raise the mower deck one last time, race up the driveway to the little metal shed where we have decided to keep the mowers, and manage to pull to a stop just short of the corrugated wall. A job well done! No serious injuries and now I can forget about quack until spring.

In Minnesota, snow can fall in any month of the year. Not that we have feet or even inches of it during the summer, but flurries and snowstorms can occur almost any time after September 1, and before May 31, and I have seen a few flakes in both June and August—never July, but I'm still young (at heart). No matter when it falls, snow almost always comes before we are ready for it, either physically or emotionally, or both.

November is just beginning to tick off its days. On each one of them I tell myself that I need to prepare the roses for winter or risk losing them altogether, yet I put it off. Part of my procrastination is that I don't exactly know what to do even if I go out there. Besides, I am in the midst of stripping wallpaper in the kitchen. It is such a huge mess that I tell myself I should not quit in the middle of it. The roses will have to wait. Or die.

On November 15, I wake up to four inches of snow. I realize that I have waited one day too many. Winter has begun. The roses are probably already dead. I pick up my scraper and my spray bottle and return to peeling paper from the kitchen walls. I remind myself that I have set my limits and I have stuck to them: I can't tackle anything outside until I finish my work inside.

The warm autumn days so beautiful for cutting down the perennials, stowing the hoses and lawn furniture, emptying pots that might break if frozen, and tilling the garden one last time, have passed me by. Some of those tasks have been done as part of the moving process, more or less. Others remain undone. Now rose care has passed me by too. In every red flower on the wallpaper, I see proof of my failures.

I scrape away wet piles of red-orange colonial print wallpaper (lots of failure reminders…) and contemplate what I have missed. Then I get honest: I have never done the autumn clean-up work on schedule anyway. I have always waited until the last possible bloom is off the last possible flower before cutting anything down or putting anything away. And, so, while most people are doing their fall gardening chores in jeans and a denim shirt, I have always done mine in Sorel boots, down jacket, long underwear, and stocking cap.

This year I've hit a new low and not done it at all. I make excuses: this is an off year—I've been busy with moving and so couldn't be expected to do everything. If the roses can't take care of themselves, they don't fit into my no-fussy-garden plan anyway. I tear into the wallpaper clean-up, and finish by nightfall with plans to prime the walls the next morning. Putting a positive spin on the situation, I tell myself winter has spared me from having to work on the roses. I tell myself I am thankful.

November 16 dawns with a bright sun. What has made me forget, I wonder, that what comes suddenly sometimes leaves just as suddenly? The ground, still warm, helps melt the snow in all but the shadiest of places. Okay, so I'm going to get a shot at the roses after all. I forget all about limits, leave the painting behind, and smile when

I find a pair of pink-and-white gardening gloves in my old coat pocket.

I walk to the garden where the sun is bright, but my fingers feel cold inside the soft cotton. Very cold. I suggest to myself that maybe I should go back to my wallpapering. After all, I had made peace with the idea of ignoring the roses yesterday. What is different about today? Besides, I still don't really know what to do with the roses, even though I purchased two boxes of the previous owner's gardening books at her auction the month before we moved in.

When I look in them for advice, I find that most of the rose books have been written by gardeners in England, where roses are to die for and winters are mild. In Minnesota, roses are mildly successful and winters are to die from. The books do not help.

A gardening friend has advised me to buy mothballs for discouraging rodents and captan to prevent fungus growth. These I carry along to the garden. I look from the first rose, which I have now identified as a hybrid tea rose, to the captan can and back again. I read the directions. I read them again. Finally, there is nothing to do but begin.

As my fingers began to freeze again, I tell myself the task will not take long and then I'll be back inside preparing the kitchen walls for new paper. I tell myself I'll just do the hybrid tea roses because the shrub roses can take care of themselves very nicely without me.

Thorns attack through the thin gloves as I begin distributing mothballs. I keep working, making a note to buy leather gloves before spring. The roses, already hardened off for winter, do not seem to want to be disturbed, yet they look cold too. I dig trenches for the hybrid tea varieties, six of them, and tip them in, marking each one with a stake and mounding them over with soil before covering them with leaves. By the time this is done, I need dry gloves. I go back to the house to get them and another box of mothballs. My fingers are stiff, but I feel very pleased with myself and decide that I can do more.

The miniature roses in the nearby bed look like the next neediest group, so I begin clipping them back, adding captan and the mothballs, then mounding them with leaves too. The smell of the captan makes me afraid that I will develop some odd cancer if I breathe too much, and so I go back to the house for a mask.

I add the mask to my stylish garden garb of pink gloves, large brown boots, mud-stained blue jeans, and my son's green-hooded, orange-and-white castoff Miami Hurricanes jacket. Just your typical country gardener, that's me. I make a

mental note to try to look more authentic in my spring gardening apparel.

The mud-stained jeans continue to grow even more stained as I crawl from bush to bush, discovering as I pull away the now frozen chickweed that there are more miniatures in the dooryard garden than I thought. I later find six more in another little patch formerly obscured by weeds that have had their livelihood depleted by the frost. I find six more in another and a whole row of them among the weeds out by the shrub roses. I run out of mothballs, and soon out of captan.

After a trip to town, and with my chemicals replenished, I go out again, this time wearing both dry jeans and dry gloves. I make my way to the place in the garden where the shrub roses grow in pleasing diagonal rows. Their leaves hang on, brown at the edges but not about to give up just because they have a little snow on them. To cut or not to cut? That is my question.

I make another trip back to the house to consult a book and, finally, find a section on winter care that offers good suggestions. In fact, it offers so many options that I bring it outside with me so that I can refer to it without having to walk all the way back up to the house with every question.

Reading a book outdoors in thirty-degree weather with a west wind blowing the pages out of my hands is a new experience for me. Oddly, it seems right. I am thankful, at last, to have a higher authority to consult. And, I find that many of these five-foot-tall shrubs need nothing from me. Some will thank me if I tie their wispy canes together so they don't whip around and break in the winter winds.

As I trudge back to the house for twine, I make a mental note to include twine in my tool basket from this time forward. I also make a mental note to *get* a tool basket before spring. And tools. Clearly a hoe alone isn't going to cut it in this garden. Ouch...

By the time I return to the shrub roses, new snow is beginning to blow in— icy flakes that cut my cheeks as I swaddle the red-twigged roses.

"We are in this together," I tell them. "I don't know much, but I'm willing to learn".

And I do have books, though perhaps I should get something on zone 4. I believe in books just as I believe in limits. Maybe even more.

This first day in the garden, I learn many important lessons. There is, of course, the old cliché: "if you don't use your head, you will have to use your feet." I do not bother to count how many trips I have made between house and garden, half of them uphill. I learn I don't need the fanciest tools for the job, but should organize the ones I have and keep them clean so as not to spread disease from rose to rose. I learn that every rose has different needs, almost a different personality, and I am astounded to realize I care about them almost as if they are children. They need me! I learn that gardening, like mowing, is more than just a summer sport. In fact, it seems even more important on that cold November day than it had during the warm autumn, because each plant is now so fragile and time so limited.

The lesson I will continue to learn each time I go to the garden, however, is: even if I don't know what I'm going to do, or how to do what I think I should do, the important thing is to go out there. To start. Do one small task: pick up sticks or pull up an errant plant. The garden will tell me what to do next. It will say: "Hey, over here! How about loosening the soil around our roots? Ahhh. That feels soooo good." And one task will lead to the next... and the next... and the next.

I realize I should be seeing this last lesson as a reason to stay out of the garden: if the garden will tell me what to do, it will never stop. That means endless work— a task that can never be done. And yet, even with the snow beginning to fall more heavily and the weeds still overrunning everything, the garden areas look as beautiful as paintings in a museum. Was Da Vinci ever done? Couldn't he always have added a few more brush strokes? Added more detail to the background? Changed the color of the sky?

Of course he could have. Perhaps later he even wished he would have. But, for one reason or another, he didn't. He might have been tired, or have had to make dinner that night, or have had company drop in. The painting is as it is, and to everyone but the artist, it looks finished. To the artist, there is always more that could be done, and yet for some reason he stops. Francis Bacon once said, "The task of the artist is to deepen the mystery," so maybe by leaving a painting unfinished the artist creates that mystery. These gardens, unfinished by any definition, are just such a mystery.

The wallpaper seems very unimportant as I walk back to the house almost four hours later. My hands have warmed up inside the thin gloves, and I have had to unzip the Hurricanes jacket a little, sweating from my flurry of November gardening. I turn my back on the garden, already thinking about being able to pick roses in the summer ahead. I will mow down the irises, but the roses stay. I am very clear on that. I will concentrate on roses. They will be my limit, my canvas, even though they too are surrounded by quack. All seventy-eight of them. And framing my canvas will be the lawn.

Did you ever wonder why plants need a dormant period? It's a survival tactic. Plants anticipate the coming of harsh conditions, like winter, by sensing decreasing light and decreasing temperatures. They then shut down their metabolic activity and conserve their energy. If they didn't, all of the water flowing through them and all of their tender new growth would freeze and kill them. Dormancy allows them to minimize the elements that would harm them, and to store nutrients for later. Plants can also go into dormancy when harsh conditions come at unexpected times (like a summer drought) in order to hold onto their precious lives so that they can revive and complete their normal yearly cycle later (think brown lawn in mid-summer that turns green again after a good rain). Even plants in climates without harsh extremes will exhibit some type of dormancy, for instance, in tropical rain forests, tree seedlings go into a state of dormancy until a break opens up in the canopy of trees above them, giving them enough light to grow to maturity. Amazing.

# 5

# Pine
# Boughs
# for a
# Nest

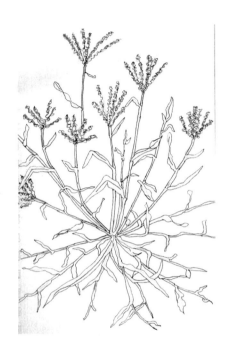

After that day of getting up close and personal with the roses, the woods and increasingly snow-covered gardens are never far from my mind as I return to work on the kitchen walls. I find myself glancing out toward the bird feeders every once in a while. When I take a break, I stand by the patio doors thinking about what to do with the gardens when winter ends and about what stroke of good fortune has settled me into this place I now call home. It is, truly, a place wished for.

I have always wanted a big, old Victorian house. I ended up with a big, contemporary house instead. It has an open stairway, but no carved newel posts like the 1880s beauties I used to dream about. It has a deck, instead of a porch with gingerbread trim. Its pantry is not for a butler, just for food. The house is large and beautifully crafted, but it is not what I ever expected to love, and yet I do.

Looking out at the jays, cardinals, juncos, and nuthatches jostling under the bird feeder, I realize that what draws me to the house is not what is inside, but what lies beyond the walls. The house has no draperies, and with the trees growing so close to the windows I feel almost like a bird on a branch. The house lets me feel like I am outside even when I'm inside.

Finally, though, that is not enough. When I finish the kitchen the first week in December, I put my painting and papering tools away. Even though there are still unpacked boxes waiting in the garage and attic, and the house is far from ready for tours, what I want to do is go outside to gather pine cones and branches for Christmas decorating. Bay windows, mantles, and ledges all need decorating, but the holiday decorations we had at the old house will not begin to fill them all. Fortunately, we now have many, *many* evergreen trees with boughs free for the taking.

The morning after a pristine five-inch snowfall, I get my red plastic sled down from its hook on the garage wall and don a pair of tall boots. The pruning shears I used on the roses are still lying near the door. I stuff them into the pocket of the puffy Hurricanes jacket that makes me look like a cross between a linebacker and a snowman, and my quest for boughs begins.

All is quiet. Birds flit from tree to tree, but there is no singing in winter. Not even a crow caws this morning. The silence is so profound that I carry the sled at first so as not to disturb anything. Brule glides noiselessly on ahead, greyhound-like, spraying up small clouds of crystals that land on her pretty brown-and-white nose.

We trek across the lawn toward the place where Scotch pines, blue spruce, and some tall evergreens I can't identify grow on the north side of the deep ravine. As I make a mental note to find out what all of these trees are, I have the immediate sense I've just added another garden task. Be careful, I tell myself. Remember your limits. They're just trees. That's all you need to know.

From the top of the ridge, all of the trees look to be about the same size. It isn't until I walk down among them that I realize the tallest deciduous trees are near the bottom of the ravine. Some of their trunks go up thirty or forty feet before they show a branch, so until I look at the ravine as a whole, I don't see what giants these low-down trees are. How deceiving are appearances, even in nature.

My plan was to clip branches from evergreens about halfway down the slope, out of sight of the lawn, where a little lopsidedness wouldn't be an issue, but those trees, too, are much larger than I'd imagined. I see immediately that my pruning shears are going to be inadequate for the branches I want.

27

I carry a few small boughs back to the house and exchange my hand pruner for a long-armed lopping pruner. Back in the ravine, I cut several big, blue, long-needled branches, reaching up to get at even the lower boughs of the trees. Whole snow banks fall down into my eyes and onto my shoulders until I learn to shake off each branch before I pull it down to my level. I feel small as a snowshoe rabbit, as if I am chewing off greens for a nest.

Deer tracks make a patterned carpet under this dense, green ceiling. Near the middle of the planting, I see the large oval imprints made by their bodies: they have been resting here in this protected place, out of the wind, out of my sight, out of my world. Feeling like an interloper, I quickly load the green branches onto the red sled. Against the white snow, the composition looks like a Christmas card, and I make a mental note to photograph it sometime and to make my own Christmas cards. Then I quickly remember I've never taken a decent picture in my life.

When the sled is heaped with boughs, I start the climb back up toward the house. Before go five feet, half of the boughs slide off. I pile them on again, being more careful to alternate the direction of the main stems this time. The sled makes a deep furrow in the snow as I pull it up the steep grade, and I am winded when I reach the top of the ravine.

When I stop to catch my breath, I look back down toward the evergreen cluster. From this angle, it looks totally untouched. Only the deer and I know it has been. I wonder if they will still want to bed down there at night now that my tracks

mingle with theirs? I wonder if I have taken too much and have been too greedy, but at the same time I wonder if I have taken enough to decorate all the places in and around the house that seem to need decorating. Suddenly, making the house look beautiful doesn't seem as important as keeping the trees happy. As I tow the greens back to the house, I make a mental note to read up on pruning evergreens, and on varieties of evergreens.

The boughs wait in the garage, drying, while I find an old milk can, a copper boiler, two five-gallon Red Wing crocks, and a couple of smaller containers. Filling these with greens is such an uncomplicated means of decorating I almost feel like I am cheating. No tinsel. No lights. No resin figurines. Just the beautiful boughs. Nothing, I feel, can improve on them. When, during the holidays, guests comment that the house looks as though we have lived in it for years, I know what makes it feel so homey—it is not what I have done, but what has been done for me by that grove of pines and by the view from every window. Nobody notices faded silver wallpaper when they can see a red cardinal sitting less than five feet on the other side of the windowpane.

As winter wears on and the snow gets deeper and deeper, I don't take time to go back into the evergreens to see if the deer are still there. I walk past the trees on my way to the mailbox and watch Brule flush a pheasant out of them now and again, but I stay on the driveway where the walking is easy.

As I hurry along, I think back to how small I felt down in the ravine under those green branches. I wonder sometimes if a deer watched me, but I did not see one. I think again that, in cutting boughs to feather my own nest, I might have disturbed someone else's and that seems wrong, but I go into denial mode. I tell myself I didn't harm a tree or creature, and that I needed the boughs. End of conversation.

Some days as Brule and I walk down the gently curving drive, the evergreens are decorated in sparkling white, some days not. It occurs to me that my attempts at decorating with boughs are meager by comparison with the effects of glittery frost on the bursts of long needles on what someone told me are eastern white pines, although I still have not made a positive IDs. One day after I come back in from my walk, I decide to find out for sure.

I have just received in the mail a two-inch thick, loose-leaf notebook filled with tree information called a Woodland Stewardship Plan. It was put together by a young man from the Minnesota Department of Natural Resources just after we moved in. He appeared at our door one day and asked if we would be interested in having a Woodland Stewardship Plan drawn up at a cost of fifty dollars. We agreed, and the young man spent considerable time walking through our woodlot, cataloging trees, and making recommendations.

The result was this wonderful notebook, which also includes lots of general information about woodlands. I flip to the section labeled "Tree Species." The pages regarding evergreens are printed on green paper to make it user-friendly for people in a hurry, like me.

Eight species are detailed in terms of appearance, management, and damaging agents. One, the red Norway pine, looks similar to the thirty- and forty-foot trees growing in the windbreak row along the road, but I am not sure. The information sheet says that red pines are to be harvested when they are eighty to 100 years old, so at least I know we will not have to cope with that, these being no more than twenty-five.

Most of the other evergreens we have are not included in the green pages. Even if they were, I know it is almost impossible, at least for me, to identify real plants from mere drawings or even photographs. Can anything in nature really be known by this kind of reproduced image? It occurs to me that plants can be known *about*, but not really known. Still, I note how the green pages show silhouettes of the different trees, called the tree form, and I try to look at individual trees with regard to their overall shape, something I have never thought about before.

The (probable) red pines have a long, branchless trunk and an irregular/triangular top section. The (probable) blue spruce have a short trunk and more conical shape. Other unknown species grow in a short, bushy manner. I am thankful to the notebook for helping me see trees in a new, more complete way. How lucky we were that the young man appeared at our door that autumn day.

I sense immediately, looking at these pages, that I want to learn not about plants in the abstract but about the living, breathing beings that prickle my fingers when I touch them, scratch my face and arms when I get too close ,and make my hands sticky with their oozing pitch. These green pages are a good start, but I need more.

Many of the trees we have appear to be non-native species. They have been planted to encourage wildlife, to discourage soil erosion, or to provide a windbreak. Some are purely ornamental. Scotch pine is one species I *can* identify because we had often had a Scotch pine Christmas tree (I continue to be amazed at the odd ways in which we come to know the world around us). For a more organized approach, I decide to check out some tree books on my next trip to the library.

In the meantime, I begin to worry about some of the pests and diseases I have learned about in the Stewardship Plan: carpenter ants and spruce budworm, schleroderris canker, and red pine shoot blight, white grubs (I saw one of these the day I tried to pull quack out of the irises), and bark beetles. What if the brown needles I see on the Scotch pines are not brown from too much winter sun reflecting off the snow as I've thought, but from one of these damaging agents?

The next time I walk by the Scotch pines on my way to the mailbox, I blow them a kiss and tell them I hope they recover from whatever is making them brown. I worry that they might not. If they don't, we'll have dozens of brown trees that will need cutting. That will mean lots of boughs, which won't really be all that useful in the middle of the summer—too much of a good thing for me, perhaps just as too much sun has harmed the pines. We can all have too much of a good thing—like too many worthwhile tasks. At least I can decide when I've had too much of a good thing and quit if I want. Evergreens are not so lucky.

Did you ever wonder if you should be part of a woodland stewardship program? Minnesota's Woodland Stewardship Program is a branch of the Land Stewardship Project, a national effort to create an awareness of the interrelationship of land and culture. It helps foster sustainable agriculture and works with corporate agriculture in developing healthy and ethical use of our earth. Woodlands programs help people learn about biodiversity in forests so that they can use and enjoy forest areas without harming them. We would never think of using a new appliance without reading the owner's manual, but we forge on out into the world without much information at all. The Land Stewardship Project can help change that. See contact information in the Appendix.

# 6

# Let There Be Peace in the Country

Evergreens enchanted me in December, but oaks get my attention in January. Every day I walk under the brown leaves still clinging to a red oak tree, whose hefty trunk leans out over the driveway. Its lower branches force every delivery truck that comes to inch up toward the house or risk: (a) being scratched and/or (b) angering the homeowner (me) if branch breakage occurs. Drivers *love* this, of course, so I make a mental note to find out when oaks should be pruned.

Studying this imposing oak each day, I begin to see why English manor houses are so often decorated with acorn and oak leaf patterns: oaks radiate strength and durability. Their acorns provide food for wildlife and so, by extension, for people. They are majestic and long lived. I have read in our Woodland Stewardship Plan that we are in what is called "oak savannah" territory, which means our area is made up of rolling hills (check—slopes everywhere on our property) over sandstone (check—we have a couple of outcroppings), but that currently most of the region is farmed (check—all of our neighbors farm, at least as a secondary occupation).

The Plan also tells me that oaks flourished in the pre-history of our region because fires from the tall-grass prairie regions surrounding us burned through here periodically and eliminated the cottonwoods and weed trees, like elms and box elders, that would have made too shady a canopy for oaks to thrive. Apparently, the mature oak trees withstood these fires, and so became the dominant species.

By now, of course, that's changed. Prairie fires are a thing of the past in this agricultural area, so now cottonwoods and all of the other trees thrive. Oaks do what they can, but I notice that our stewardship advisor has indicated it would be a good idea to "release," meaning "cut," a number of large cottonwoods within the next ten years.

Even in the depths of winter, the red oaks, at least, hold their leaves. I see them every day, their leaves imprinting the fresh snow if they fall, though most don't. They rustle in the winter wind like sheets of crisp paper. Then one day in the spring, I know they will give it all up, drop as if someone has emptied several bushel baskets, and start making new leaves again. *Quercus*.

I know the Latin name for the genus because Brule's sire was named Quercus and the owner told me that all of the dogs in her line were named for species of oaks. I make a mental note to learn more Latin names for plants.

As it happens, just across the driveway from the leaf-covered oak lie the four offending rows of shorn quack and their demeaned cousins the irises, peonies, and daylilies. Every time I walk past, I try to arrive at some good solution for these problem children. Maybe in the spring I should not mow them down until after I have let them flower once?

This comes to me as I am on a twelve-foot ladder painting my bedroom. I tell myself that I am tempting fate to even think that the flowers will look like much among all of that quack, but the idea lingers. At least by seeing one bloom cycle, I will know what is worth saving. Will I be able to stand looking at the surrounding quack? That is the question.

At that moment, in late afternoon with daylight dwindling, I cannot stand to look at my bedroom walls. My first attempt at sponge painting them has been a terrible failure. I somehow forgot that, for this technique to succeed, one should use colors close in value. I, instead, have used dark-blue and off-white. The effect is like being inside of a graniteware washtub.

I add another layer of the white, covering most of the blue and call it good, eager to apply the Carol Endres wallpaper border of folk art angels whose trumpets carry banners that say, "Let there be peace in the country." The beauty of the border almost makes up for the misery of the paint, but not quite. I try the old trick of telling myself that there are three things I like about the paint. Unfortunately, I am unable to tell myself what they are. Just as it is getting dark, I leave it all behind and bundle into the Miami Hurricanes jacket to go out for a walk with Brule. At the last minute, I decide to buckle on my snowshoes too.

Outside it doesn't seem as dark as it looked from inside. My eyes adjust and I listen to the clumsy *thwack, thwack, thwack* of the long wooden snowshoes as I make my way around the unplowed portion of the drive and out onto the lawn. The moon, just coming up, is almost full, so close I feel I might be able to snowshoe right up to it. The trees at the edge of the woods are shapes more than types in this light, and I notice a burl on one, probably an oak by the look of its gnarled branches.

Light streams out of the bedroom windows, clearly exposing my big orange and yellow ladder—and the paint, which doesn't look any better from a distance than it did up close. I consider howling at the moon.

The snow crunches under me in the negative-fifteen-degree cold. I cannot keep Brule out for long in this brutal temperature, I think, but so far she doesn't mind and has already run down near the quack rows. Are mice and voles hanging out there even after I ran the John Deere over them? Brule certainly finds something interesting there.

The rows rise like low mountain ranges under the snow and even cast a long, narrow shadow in the moonlight. It is really quite beautiful. Beautiful enough to make me think that I should let them flower in the spring. I could mow the iris spears down or dig a few out later. For now, the moon reminds me that things take on a different appearance in a different light. (I know my bedroom walls will look better once the lights are off.) The burled oak reminds me that some mistakes turn out to be beautiful (bedroom walls notwithstanding).

I look behind me at the even herringbone of my snowshoe tracks in the snow. Standing still, I hear no *thwack-thwack*. I see no quack. I try to picture the irises in bloom, and I wonder about the Latin name for iris and peony. Quack probably had one too—even Rome wasn't quack free, I am certain. The red oak by the driveway holds me in its weblike dark shadow while the rest of the lawn basks in the shimmer of the Wolf Moon. The cold is almost forgotten: the scene is breathtaking (in the non-lung-searing sense of the word).

Looking at it all, I realize I have left the disappointment of the bedroom paint job behind me. I am thankful for the restorative power of a good walk, the friendship of a dog, the warmth of an old coat, the light of a hungry moon, and the ability of snowshoes to lift me above the deep snow that would otherwise have filled my boots after the first two steps—the Minnesota version of walking on water, I decide. Truly, there is peace in the country. And for a few moments, I think I might have found it. In any language. *Pax.*

Did you ever wonder about the many names for the full moon? Native peoples on every continent watched the moon's journey and found it even more fascinating than the sun because of its constant change. Besides the Wolf Moon and the Snow Moon, some Native Americans called March the Worm Moon (earthworms begin work), April the Grass Moon (and I guess we know what that one means). May is known as the Flower Moon, June as the Strawberry Moon, July as the Buck Moon (male deer lose the velvety covering on their horns), and August is the Red Moon (because it often rises through a red haze). In September we have the Corn Moon (when corn should be harvested) which can also be called the Harvest Moon. The October moon is also called the Harvest Moon, rising large and golden and unforgettable. November brings the Beaver Moon (time to trap beavers) and December gives us the Cold Moon (self-explanatory). Other cultures have other names. You might like to make up your own list as you watch the moon travel your sky. For an added challenge: learn them in Ojibawa.

# 7

# Making Tracks

P aul Gruchow, in his book *Grassroots: The Universe of Home*, speaks of things that have gone before us:

The remarkable thing, in fact, is that one finds so few bones. Millions of creatures die every day. Where are their remains? Where have they all gone? And as for the dying creatures, where are they? You can walk for a thousand miles and never once see a creature dying. Death is nothing if not discrete. The bones, every one, are miracles, the alms nature offers to life. It is hard to believe in miracles. They seem to fall beyond the boundaries of cause and effect. But a miracle is nothing more than a story that begins after the event. It is the mysterious space between the particles of a story, like the space between the particles of an atom, that makes the substance of things possible. The miracle of a bone is that it is the evidence of something particular that once lived, something unprecedented, and never to be repeated, that has vanished yet nevertheless endures in bone, a faint white glimmering, in some offhand place, of life everlasting.

Tracks, though we find them often, are even less permanent, but offer similarities to the bones Gruchow talks about. Tracks in the snow tell us that something has gone before us, maybe even just a few seconds before us, though we cannot know when, even if we grew up believing the Lone Ranger's sidekick, Tonto, who could always tell if a bad guy's tracks were two hours or two days old.

When I finally feel competent enough to navigate between trees on my snowshoes, I begin to walk into the woods in the early morning to see what has passed through during the night. At first it is enough just to see different sorts of tracks, but soon I need to know what they are. I try remembering what they looked like and then looking them up in the encyclopedia when I come back in the house, but this is about as helpful as trying to identify a seventy-five-foot-tall pine tree from a one-inch high drawing.

One day I find a copy of *Track Pack: Animal Tracks in Full Life Size* by Ed Gray in a local bookstore. It is a pocket-size, spiral-bound book that not only shows the paw print, but also the rhythm of the tracks—maybe four close together followed by a space and then four more like the marten, or a continuous chain like the muskrat. It also shows both fore and hind feet, which make me realize that I have never thought much about that particular distinction, just as I have not paid enough attention to the difference between a red oak and a white oak. How much there is to learn, and how little time.

I zip *Track Pack* into an inner pocket in the Hurricanes jacket and am eager to pull it out after the first dusting of snow that might reveal nighttime visitors, or even daytime ones, because I already know that I do not see most of what goes on in the woods by day. To do that, I will have to sit quietly for hours, like the photographer Jim Brandenburg did to obtain his one perfect shot per day in his inspiring book, *Chased by the Light.* While I would love to do that, I am still, unfortunately, toiling away at home renovation—now the dining room.

In any case, the first time I pull out *Track Pack*, I realize that it is not going to be a panacea either. I see tracks that look like what the book says are skunk tracks, but I know that skunks are supposed to be hibernating now. They can't be out already? Can they? If they are—oh, dear. The book includes tracks for species we

do not have in southeastern Minnesota, like lynx and mountain goat, but I check these out, wanting to be ready if I ever see anything like that in my woods.

Comparing tracks in the snow to drawings of tracks by the artist DeCourcy L. Taylor, Jr., who illustrated *Track Pack,* proves not only difficult, but also makes me wonder how anyone can be sure of a set of tracks. *Are some of the people who say they are sure really not all that sure?* I begin to suspect this might be the case, yet I chide myself for my unwillingness to make a firm diagnosis from the information presented. Why do I insist on perfection? I suspect even Tonto allowed fifteen minutes one way or the other in advising the Lone Ranger.

I get hung up on the knowledge that tracks in a dusting of snow are different from tracks in deep snow. Tracks in mud, I already know, will be different from tracks in snow. And what is the big deal about tracks anyway? Who cares?

Like Gruchow, I care. I find a miracle in the lives that have gone before us and that seem to live parallel to us, because life in this woodland is teaching me that we aren't parallel at all—we are all in it together. I want to know about the wild turkey, and the squirrel, and badger, and opossum because they live here with me. Their food comes from the same soil mine does. We breathe the same air. It seems only reasonable, then, that we should at least have some sense of each other's schedules and habits so we can stay out of each other's way—or maybe even get used to each other (this would be especially beneficial if it allows me to keep from screaming every time I see something move). So far, though, I am better with tracks than with the actual animals. We all have our limits.

As the snow begins to melt on a few south slopes in the woods, I look not just for tracks, but for bones, wondering if Gruchow was right. I know that deer must die in our woods, along with zillions of other woodland creatures. Can I look at things carefully enough to find bones?

I begin to walk even more bent over than I have while examining tracks, but I come up empty. It occurs to me that it would be great to find a set of deer antlers in the woods, but that, too, eludes me. What is the secret of all of this besides the fact that other animals feed on old bones and antlers? How does nature so quickly receive these alms that I can't even see them offered? Just when I think I am getting to know a thing or two about the woods, I find out that I don't really know much at all.

If we humans are ever foolish enough to think that we are somehow separate from, or better than the natural world, we need to think again. No matter where we walk or what we see or don't see, someone or something has gone before us. Maybe it is a person, maybe a tyrannosaurus rex, maybe a gooseberry bush, or the lowly poison ivy. It has been there and in some form remains there still. Our footprints are not the first and will not be the last, no matter how hard we try to make the world our own private colony.

Each day I see less and less snow in the woods. Here and there bits of green begin to poke through. Once again I am reminded that the plants I take for granted underfoot are mostly unknown to me. I read in our Stewardship Plan that among the rare animals in our oak savannah region are the loggerhead shrike, the wood turtle, and Blanding's turtle.

Needless to say, *Track Pack* does not concern itself with these rare species. Tracking them down will require skills far beyond my own, but I can try to create a habitat that will encourage them. I will have to make tracks if I am ever going to accomplish all the tasks on my lengthening list. But should I? Can I?

I manage to turn around on my snowshoes and head back toward the house without hooking either the toe end or the tail end on a tree and falling down. Looking back, I see that I've made a pinwheel design in the snow. Nice. What kills me is that every creature in the woods will know what my tracks are without having to refer to a book. And they probably know, too, that one thing that has gone before us is quack.

Did you ever wonder how to find deer antlers in the woods? Called antler sheds, they are sought after by collectors for their beauty, but also for use as buttons and decorative items. The best time to look is in the early spring, just after the antlers have been shed, because soon after they hit the ground field mice will begin to chew on them for their calcium (everybody takes calcium, right?) Dogs can be specially trained to hunt for antlers (Brule has not taken this course). Maybe the best way to find antlers is not to look at all. Just hike woods and fields as much as you can for the sheer enjoyment of it. One day an antler may find you. (I am still waiting for this happy surprise.)

# 8

# Curves and Cosmetics

When we get a couple of fifty-degree days in March, I start to walk around the edges of the deeply wet garden spaces and search for signs of life. Some unidentified perennials oblige, and the annual spring garden excitement begins. April arrives with a couple of sixty-degree days, and I realize I actually have an even more pressing worry than quack: there is no place to plant a vegetable garden.

On the first seventy-degree day, I get out the garden hose. Everything is still soaked from the melted snow, so I don't need to water—the hose is part of my "by the book" gardening plan. One of my resources tells me the hose works well for laying out pleasing curves. The nice green line makes it easy to see how a possible new area will look, and can be lifted and changed in a moment's time.

Since this seems preferable to digging up a huge area and finding it doesn't look the way one had planned, I load up 150 feet of hose in the wheelbarrow and drop it beside the long row of irises. The long rows form an S curve, and following that would make some sense, but it just doesn't seem to have the right eye appeal. After moving the hose a few times, I opt for a teardrop-shaped area alongside the row of irises.

Step two requires a little more effort than the hose step. It requires the use of my best butcher's knife and considerable time on my hands and knees. First I cut around the teardrop with my knife, and then I cut the area into strips about eighteen inches wide. Then begins the work that is the beginning of an ongoing case of tendonitis, in both arms, the actual cutting off of the sod.

The special angle involved in getting the knife blade parallel with the earth is no doubt the cause of the injury, but I don't even notice it at first. All I see is how beautiful the soil looks with the sod gone, and how beautiful my stack of sod pieces looks, neatly rolled beside the garden with absolutely no practical use in sight. Tendonitis or not, I carve away at the new garden space where I convince myself there will be no weeds, even though tell-tale white roots lurk like worms in the brown soil. I keep right on cutting. Five hours later, I am done, and my right hand is numb. I assume this will go away.

By the next day, I am ready to give the teardrop garden a good, deep tilling to aerate it and help it dry for planting. The little red tiller inches easily through the soil, like a mixer in chocolate cake batter. I shiver with delight at every quack root chopped to bits. Soon the space is fluffed to a moist and fertile-looking brown that perfumes the damp spring air: a gardener's ambrosia.

The soil is tilled to within a foot of the iris row, and I decide to have a go with the shovel to see if it might be easier than I think it will be to dig out a few rhizomes. The surrounding quack, already getting green, is so tightly interwoven that I make no headway. The iris spears and peony shoots are beginning to assert themselves, daylilies too. The fourth row, which earlier appeared to be all quack, now appears to be some kind of super quack with thick, dark shoots.

As spring unfolds, I am surprised and delighted by all that comes up in my new world. Daffodils spring through in at least twenty places in the woods along the driveway and in some flower beds close to the house. Miniature and full-sized tulips emerge. Some blue flowers, which after some research I identify as *Scilla,* drift across the ground below holly and cotoneaster shrubs. Crocuses pop up in several beds, along with grape hyacinths, azaleas, rhododendrons, alliums, and yellow bellwort. Rose bushes I haven't seen before present themselves for my approval among wild geraniums that blanket the gardens and woods with a soft purple. I am in awe.

With April comes Daylight Saving Time, causing dawn to come an hour later on the clock. No matter what time the clock says, I, who have always loved sleeping late, find myself eager to get up in the morning and get to the garden while the day is cool. Dawn amazes me with its quiet power, its vibrant yellows and golds and pinks, and with its beautiful, soft light. The sun and I have our jobs to do: we both have to rise to the occasion.

Alas, I am not as predictable as the sun, yet most days find me in the garden early, contemplating the cosmic from my microcosmic plot of earth. I think of Shakespeare's phrase "rosey-fingered dawn," and know that Will did not spend every morning sleeping off the previous night's performance.

The powerful morning sunlight manages to draw every tree on the edge of the woods toward the east. They bend in graceful arcs toward the sun, knowing from experience that they have to reach for the light. Beneath them, buds swelling on dozens of shrubs finally reveal themselves as lilacs. By the middle of May, white, lavender, and pink blossoms bathe me in their scent during my garden mornings. I thank my lucky stars that no matter how poor my gardening attempts, and no matter what happens with the irises, at least I have indestructible and ever-reliable lilacs. At least in spring I will have bouquets.

Morning sun gives way to a stronger statement from the sun, one that reminds me that I need to buy a giant economy-size bottle of sun screen the next time I go to the store. When I get up from weeding in the sun and move into the shade, I am struck by how much relief the big trees give, arching over the garden on the west side. I worry it might be too shady for my proposed vegetable garden. Why didn't I think of that when I was laying things out with the hose? Spring tricked me, its trees leafless and bare, and made me assume that what was sunny then would be sunny in summer. Already in May, I can see another assumption gone wrong.

Nevertheless, with the new vegetable area delineated and the last frost date fast approaching, I finally take time to wonder how I will actually plant vegetables in a space shaped like a teardrop. In rows? Hills? Why was I seduced by that gentle curve of the garden hose anyway? Because my gardening books told me to do it that way, I suppose, and I neglected to realize they were talking about flower gardens, or areas for shrubs. I am planting vegetables. I decide to plant in rows.

The first row is only two feet long, but it is still a row—of basil, which doesn't require a twenty-foot row. I plant the rest—beets, pole beans, tomatoes, peppers, dill, and a few hills of potatoes. The whole look can either be called questionable, or charming. I choose charming.

Then comes the first week in June. A row of bright yellow irises and peonies in white, pink and dark red, and purple Siberian irises (there *is* a fourth row!) rush to out-bloom each other while the daylilies wait their turn. I have never before in my life found myself among so many flowers. I cannot mow them down. Or simply settle for one of each. I am going to have to keep them all. And I will have to somehow get rid of the quack.

"Cosmetic weeding" seems to be the answer. My tendonitis being what it has come to be, I know I can't pull out all of the quack (*and* the Canadian thistles *and* dandelions *and* other weeds I find also very prolific) in any kind of eradication effort, so I settle for just allowing the weeds to break below the soil level as they will.

I spend hours sitting on the ground, sometimes lying on the ground, just tearing away at the weeds. When I take the time to look up and see the bearded faces of the irises as larger than myself, I am humbled. And yet when I walk along beside the cosmetically weeded row and look down into those same faces, I do not feel superior. I feel a sense of camaraderie with my wonderful new friends, even though I am taller. We are working together, these irises and I.

From up close, the cosmetic weeding is a success only for about a day. From the driveway and from the road another fifty yards away, the whole thing looks quite nice for close to two weeks: the green grass thoroughfare between the rows sets them off like a well-tended English garden. The tiny vegetable/flower garden begins to emerge off to one side. I make a twig fence for the pole beans to climb in order to add some height to an otherwise diminutive array. The roses begin blooming in great mounds of pink and white and red almost at the same time the irises bloom.

I spend some early mornings just sitting quietly amid the mass of colors, smelling the subtle scents, feeling the touch of the soft petals on my arms and legs. When we talk about being touched by something, we usually don't mean being literally touched, but in this garden, with its stately, tall irises, I encounter both the literal and figurative. My admiration of the irises' determination against forces like wind, weather, and spaniels, which could so easily defeat them, their array of colors, the drape of their petals, their unique fragrance, and their knowing of their place in the world all rise in me and bring me to a moment of realization: I am going to maintain a garden considerably larger than I ever imagined.

As soon as I see what is in store for me, I question myself. I question my ability to do it all, and especially my ability to do it all right. I decide I will keep on with the cosmetic approach and just do the best I can. Maybe I can have it both ways? I can have the rows of flowers in June and just sort of "get by" the rest of the year? I am not really sure what I am doing, but I find I can't wait to get out to it each morning.

How large should a garden be? This I ask myself over and over, fearing that if I make this garden too big, I will never be able to take care of it. Already I fear I made the vegetable garden too small, despite my best attempts at planning things out with the hose. As I consider the size of the potential perennial garden, I decide that my previous gardens suffered from being too small rather than from being too large. The larger the space, the more room the plants have to thrive, as these irises and their companions are thriving.

Larger spaces offer more options for color arrangements. New plants can be auditioned. The more plants we grow, the greater our chances for success, no matter how we define the word. So, I rationalize that I can make a garden of these four long rows of weedy perennials, with their teardrop vegetable garden appendage, because that is what seems to be called for in this place.

Gardens are, in many ways, about numbers. Numbers of growing days in the season, numbers of seeds in a packet, numbers of inches of rainfall, degrees of temperature, feet in lengths of rows, inches in heights of plants. All numbers. I am glad, at last, that I once, long ago, paid attention in math class. At one time I thought the only important numbers in a garden were how many tomatoes I grew or how many pounds of potatoes I harvested, but in this flower garden I realize it isn't the totals that count.

The flower garden is not about yields. It is about ecstasy. I see the bliss in one rose every bit as much as in the five hundred Siberian irises. Yet, I face a row of hundreds of iris blooms of all kinds, and I do some quick arithmetic to see how many hours it will take me to: (a) make it look like an actual garden, and (b) maintain it once it becomes a garden. The sum: many, many hours.

When the John Deere garden tractor comes roaring alongside the row of fading irises a couple of weeks later, it does not touch the four problem rows. It does not even go between them. This task requires the more delicate touch of the push mower. It leaves much quack unharmed and I know a huge challenge lies ahead, yet something tells me that I have to take it. On this new property, we have accepted a gift, along with a responsibility. We will probably have to fight our way through it like irises growing up through the quack. Yet, we take the leap of faith that says, "You can do it."

Walt Whitman wrote in *Leaves of Grass*: "Now I see the secret of making the best persons. It is to grow in the open air, and to eat and sleep with the earth." *Leaves of Grass.* The title alone makes my heart race. Yet I have already seen, in these early weeks in the garden, that something very good is happening to me, despite the quack.

As I observe the natural world, I learn about the plants, but I learn more about myself. I have time to think. The garden is a doorway that allows me to come into the natural world. But even as I bask in the wonderful company of my plants, I sense that the garden is not the only doorway. It just happens to be the one open for me at a time when I am ready to step through it.

Life, of course, isn't always an open door. Sometimes it is more like a thick woodlot. Saplings scratch our faces and vines trip us. Fallen trees force us to change our route. Underbrush obscures the path. Every woodlot by definition comes with open spaces where the canopy ends, where the oaks thrive, where gardens grow.

Most of us will leave a woodlot with a new affection because we have left part of ourselves in there. We might have left confusion, or a tissue that escaped our pocket. We might have cut a tree, or planted one. We might have discarded a wrong idea for a right one. If we were lost, we might laugh at our own stupidity. On the

other hand, we might feel ourselves fill up with pride at what we have learned. There is so much in the world we do not know, so much unexplained. So it is with the garden. Especially in spring.

Did you ever wonder what makes a seed planted below the soil level grow up instead of down? After all, how does it know? No matter which direction it goes, it is still in the soil. Amazingly enough, you aren't the only one who wonders about this. Scientists are not totally in agreement about what happens, either. They do know, however, that plants use chemical signals to grow toward the light, which is called "phototropism." Plant physiologists know that this is caused by a hormone called auxin, but do not know exactly how it works. Looking for a new frontier? Plants are waiting for you.

# 9

# From the Mountain to the Valley

In spring when it is too cold and wet to work in the gardens, it is not too cold and wet for garage sales. Though I have become busy with the gardens, I have not been purged of the need to collect that made the big house so attractive in the first place. I see a Ford Ranger pickup advertised in an estate sale ad. I know the truck and I knew its driver, a woman I admired very much. Before her untimely death, she had embraced the world, spending much of her life doing wonderful things for other people. I suppose that somewhere, deep inside, I hope the truck will help me to be like her, but that is not part of Ford's guarantee.

Nevertheless, no more than two hours later, I own a well-used, but still sharp-looking, black, four-wheel-drive truck that will be perfect for hauling plants and peat moss and whatever else might be needed in reclamation projects.

I will now have something big and powerful in my arsenal of garden tools, something essential to my war with quack: my own little Sherman tank. Now there will be no excuse for not getting down to business on the quack eradication in the long rows east of the house, my own "Eastern Front." Do I pause to consider what happened to Napoleon on his eastern front? Of course not. I only see I will be able to haul away every bit of quack I am going to eradicate, along with assorted small tree weeds (box elders and elms, mostly) and brush.

There is one small problem with the new purchase: the truck has a standard transmission and, although I took my driver's training behind a stick, I never mastered shifting. Not even close. When I look at the truck, I remember the humiliation of my driving instructor's comments as I killed the engine repeatedly on the steep hill where he had me practice. He finally gave me a passing grade just to get me out of his class. I was able to take my test in my parents' automatic, and if hadn't, I would probably still not have a license.

No, I never mastered the hill start, and now we live on top of a hill. I know that the truck will send me lurching back and forth from garden to brush pile, and that the neighbors might hear me grinding the gears. I prepare myself for comments on my lack of skills. I promise myself to improve said skills. I do not promise when.

When we leave the sale, my husband drives the truck home. I can't imagine why. I take the car and drive on to another sale where I find a hat. A twenty-five-cent straw model, its brim is broken apart on one side so that the rapidly unweaving straw is escaping in all directions. The hatband is gone, but two large pink silk roses remain.

When I buy it I am certain it will be just right: its brim wide enough to provide plenty of shade despite the injury. I think I look quite good in it too, fulfilling part of last fall's promise to upgrade my gardening apparel. A novice hat wearer, I fail to take into account how it will perform in the wind: The hat spends more time cartwheeling across the grass than on my head.

When I try a baseball cap, I quickly realize it will not shade my neck. I buy yet another straw hat, one tied under the chin. Too hot. Still, I need a good hat. Gardeners have always needed them, and not just for style. Sun is the gardener's friend, and enemy. A hat keeps things positive all around.

A week later, I find a hat that makes me appreciate anew all the things connecting us in the universe. The hat, called a *topee* or *pith helmet*, has an inner, adjustable band that allows it to fit securely and an inner framework that keeps the

outer covering up and away from my head. Think of British officers in the heat of India or Africa and the image of the topee comes to mind. Or think of Meryl Streep on safari with Robert Redford in *Out of Africa*—hers was trimmed with tulle, and she set it aside so that Redford could wash her hair in a leather basin out on the veld. Well, nobody needs a topee all the time.

On the first day I wear the hat, I discover what the British Army knew all along: the hat serves a multitude of good purposes, namely that it does not blow off in the wind (even without the chin strap) and that it protects the face, ears, and neck from the hot sun. It does, however, give "hat hair." My family is not amused by the way I look when I come in from the garden, hair plastered to the crown of my head. I wear the hat anyway, because it works, and I remind them that if they had to toil in the sun as I do, they would be begging to borrow my topee.

Yet it isn't to soldiers that I feel connected as the terrycloth-lined sweatband of the hat seats itself on my head. It is to my father, who also owned a topee. His was dark-green canvas, U.S. Army issue, something he had picked up at a surplus store and probably paid fifty cents for, just as I have for mine. He bought his topee on a lark, then realized, no doubt, how practical and useful it was, just as I have. He wore it for a good number of years—until a tree fell on it one day when he was helping a neighbor log off a section of woodland (and yes, he was in it at the time, but a branch knocked it off and *then* the tree smashed it). I hope mine will not be subjected to such abuse in our woodlot. If it is, I hope I will be able to see as much humor in it as my father did.

Arsenal of tools and military hat. I am at war with quack, which is now also rearing its ugly head in my carefully de-sodded vegetable plot, giving new meaning to the name "teardrop" garden. I have always thought of myself as a peace-loving individual, and so I am surprised at how quickly I revert to the language of war when my own little piece of the world is challenged. I tell myself that my war is only language, but somewhere deep inside I know it isn't just terminology. Though no shots will be fired, I am going to be very much at war with quack. Like every good patriot, I promise to conquer it or die trying, although I do not promise when or how.

The topee, or pith helmet, is named for the style (helmet) and what it was made from (the pith of sola, a swamp plant in India). Later on the hats were made from cork and covered with white or tan fabric, but they were still called pith helmets. One model was even nicknamed "The Bombay Bowler." Military topees (also spelled topi, from the Indian word), especially after World War I, were often made of lightweight metal covered with khaki canvas. The hatband is known as a puggaree, and all models feature eyelets to help vent heat out from the crown. Whatever the material, this was the headgear of choice for westerners in the tropics from the mid-1850s when Europe began to have colonies in India and Africa. It remains in limited use for gardeners, hikers and safari travelers, though many feel it to be appropriate only as part of a costume. Hmmm.

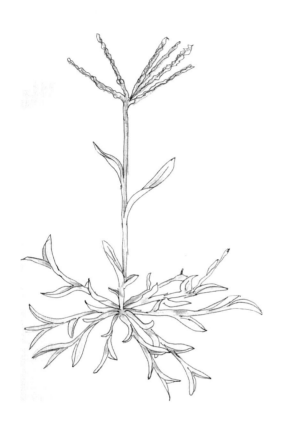

# 10

# On My Knees

I might be waging war, but I long for peace. Attaining peace with quack, however, seems impossible. Quack, for example, is determined to thrive at all costs. And I am determined to conquer it at all costs. A book on feng shui tells me weeds must be removed from the garden to create a feeling of peace. In the shade of my new topee, I look out across the newly cut grass and feel peace until I see the battlefield of quacky irises, the quacky peonies, ditto daylilies, and Siberians. In this war, quack appears to be winning.

Maybe that's why, when we take a weekend off and drive to Lake Superior's south shore where we have a cabin, I am struck even more than I usually am at the peacefulness of that place. The lake, of course, has a less-than-peaceful reputation. Its ability to change from mirror to monster on the breath of a breeze is well documented. Its cold water, having an average temperature of forty-two degrees in the summer, will destroy the peace of one's body temperature if one goes for a swim. Still, its sunsets, unknowable depths, and unpredictable personality pour themselves into the soul in a way that brings indescribable peace.

When I was a child just learning how to tell agates from other kinds of rocks, I walked along the beach, looking down at the ridge of small stones rinsed by the waves. Agates, because they are translucent, sparkle in the sunlight, especially when wet. I never even looked at the rocks beyond the reach of the waves—they were dull, brown and not at all interesting. When I was older, I realized that if I bent over I could get a better look and find more agates, even among the dry stones. And, if I was really serious, I got down on my hands and knees.

One summer the lake currents changed and not so many rocks washed up onto our beach. I had already plundered those easy for the taking and my parents didn't want to drive to another beach. The only other option was to look in the lake itself. Lying on my tummy with my head out over the end of an air mattress, I would paddle along in the shallow water and look down. Many rocks showed promise, especially if the lake was completely still, but I never found more than one or two small chips in all my many tries. Quartz was especially annoying because it, too, is translucent and appears agate-like when wet. I would pick up agate look-alikes and then fire them off out into the deep water so that they could not fool me again. Some days my right arm actually got tired from throwing so many rocks into deep water.

Despite agate failure, I learned that all of the rocks were beautiful when down under the water. Everything sparkled. Eventually I decided the best thing to do was to leave them alone so that someone else could take a closer look too.

Lake Superior, for me, is both mystery and open book. When it is calm, it appears to tell all, but it can toss up three-foot waves without a minute's notice. As a child, I was determined to learn all its secrets. Now I am more intrigued by its mystery.

Because the lake's essential nature has been unchanged in the last several thousand years, I can walk along its shores and envision those who built fires on the sand and watched the stars, the magnificent sunsets, the storms beginning to brew. I can call up the stories of Swedish immigrants rafting out from Duluth to reach their new homesteads. I can imagine both the peace they found when they came into that world, and the war they waged against stumps and grasshoppers and the terror of losing children to diphtheria or rheumatic fever so far away from a doctor. The lake is circled by unmarked graves, and a few marked ones too, from the early days when somebody stood in awe of that beauty, defenseless against that power, just as I do.

Lake Superior is one of those places where it is actually nice to be on a rainy day, or a snowy one. The lake commands its own little weather system, and when it starts raining it can go on for days, the clouds anchored by all that water below. In winter, snowflakes form and reform via evaporation. When storms roll in, everything goes into slow motion. People still work, still go about their jobs, but there is a sense that some things just won't be done until the weather clears. Admitting that frees people to do something else, or to do nothing but get to know themselves a little better. They may complain about the weather. They may curse the weather. But somewhere, deep inside is a place that *likes* that weather, the damp cold that makes a person want to rush into a warm house and have a cup of coffee, or down to the local bar to find some friends with whom to curse the weather and then laugh about it, to sit down and read a book from one's own library, a book set aside for just such a day.

Weather can make everything normal beyond reach, out of people's control—and that admission is freeing to people reared to believe they must always be "in control." The lake does that. Mountains do that in other places. Rivers do it. Oceans do it. Woodlands do it. Nature does it. These places exude peace.

Quack does not. Yet, quack greets me first when I get back home to the garden. I ignore it, even cover up for it by mowing and making the whole lawn look so beautiful that most don't even notice the quacky, long rows. Our children usually mow the bulk of the lawn with the John Deere so that I only have to trim around the gardens with the push mower, which is still an hour's work. I know where things are planted and where quack hides under drooping foliage. I get up close to the perennials, roses, and vegetable garden, mowing away all of the quack I can. The freshly cut strips of lawn between the four problem rows look almost presentable. Almost.

As I trim along the edge of the shade garden with our trusty Lawn Boy in late June, something catches my eye a couple of feet ahead of the mower. I manage to halt before I get to it and there, sure enough, growing in the grass, I see what looks like a tiny hosta. I hold back for a moment, afraid it might be a plantain, but finally I get down on hands and knees for a closer look and decide to take a chance. If it turns out to be a weed, I have wasted nothing but a little time.

Most people would shut off the mower at this point, dig up the plant and then finish mowing later, but I have a great deal of trouble pulling the starter cord and so

never stop for anything. I swing the mower out a couple of feet from the garden and finish mowing the whole lawn, leaving a strip of uncut grass I figure I can get somebody else to do later—like my tall son, who can always start the mower on the first pull.

By the time I am done mowing, two or three hours later, the hosta possibility is already forgotten. It is not until I get back to the house to look out with pride on my handiwork that I see the unsightly swatch of shaggy green next to the shade garden. Better late than never. I get a hand digger and go out for a closer look.

It is late evening by this time and slices of sunlight thin as window glass cut through the shadows of trees between me and the sun. As I kneel down, just before the dew begins to fall, I wonder if I will even find the little plant again—it was less than a half-inch in any direction. But I find it right away, the shine of its leaf as distinct from the shine of the grass as silver is distinct from gold, and I am just about to dig in when I see another. And another. And another and another and another.

Now I am certain it's plantain. No good plant reproduces itself like this, I tell myself. These have to be weeds. I know there is a rather large, unsightly plantain growing not far away—we have far from a weed-free lawn—and so I get up and walk over the damp grass to check it out. The plantain just isn't the same, not the way the leaves present

56

themselves, not the veining, not the color—none of it. I know, of course, that young plants are not always smaller pictures of their parents. Like people, plants change as they grow up, and change again as they age and finally die, but still there is the essence of their future in them, even as seedlings. This plantain is not like the tiny seedlings just a few feet away in the grass next to the hosta border.

And so I go back, poking the end of my trowel in and scooping out the tiny plants until I again convince myself that they *must* be weeds. That by digging them up I have been so stupid I will be laughed at by any real gardener who comes to visit. I do not, however, have to convince myself that digging these plants up is leaving numerous holes in our lawn—I can see that for myself.

Becoming truly apprehensive about my aptitude for this kind of work, not to mention tired, I stop. I do not need them all, even if they are all hostas. Besides, it's getting dark. What will I do with forty more hostas? I already have dozens of them. And maybe these are not even hostas. What do I know, anyway?

I take my booty around to the other side of the house where I shovel a little loose dirt into a flat, cardboard box and set in the questionable apparitions. Sprinkling them with water and covering them with a damp towel, I leave for the night. If they are weeds they'll still be growing in the morning, I tell myself. If they are dead, I'll know they were hostas.

In the morning, I lift the towel from the box, and there they are, still shiny and apparently none the worse for wear after their crude upheaval from a cozy life amid the protection of the grass. In fact, they look happy to be away from it. They also look amazingly like hostas. And so, I set off with the box and plant hostas wherever I find an empty space, bordering places that do not need bordering just so the little plants will have a home in places safe from both the lawn mower and my propensity to forget what is planted where and subsequently to rip it out by the roots.

A box half full of tiny hostas remains. These I pot in leftover greenhouse containers. Each little plant in its two-inch container takes on a completely different look. I see them as more worthy, somehow. I see them as individuals. I see them as signs of hope. After all, plants from the greenhouse have come in these containers and gone on to become gorgeous, huge plants. Setting these little two-leafed wonders in those pots gives them the same cachet. There is only one problem: once in those pots, these plants are just too nice to plant anywhere.

So, I line them up in a row on the cement outside the chain link dog kennel fence, a narrow ledge just large enough for them. Every time I walk past, I marvel at them as if they are a long, narrow window box garden. They take right off and grow in that shady spot, and since the dog almost never is placed in the kennel because she feels lonely out there, they are not even subject to dog breath or any other hazards of nature. They thrive in peace.

Their brothers and sisters, who found their way directly into the soil, do not so much thrive as hang on. They seem to stay the same, not dying but not really growing either. I mark each of them with a plastic fork just so I won't forget them, and for a while I tell myself that, if they die, I can always replace them with the ones from the pots.

But they do not die. They hang on. I cannot think of any more places to plant hostas short of digging up more earth for flower beds, and so I give away the potted ones. To anyone who will take them go the tiny ambassadors. Some people who do not even really want them are too polite to say no and take home the tiny plants instead.

When there are just six left, I finally give up and plant them in between the six tiny boxwoods my sister has given me—seedlings that had grown in her garden. I decide that the twelve of them will have something to talk about, at least, since my sister is not only a boxwood propagator, but also, in my book, the queen of hostas. She owns dozens, knows them all by their Latin names and, best of all, she shares. The slow-growing boxwoods will protect the tiny hostas from harm but will not overpower them the way another hosta might.

I do not really know which hosta was responsible for seeding these, and so I don't know how large they might end up. I don't actually care. I just keep watching them. Each week I see more signs that they are, in fact, hostas and not any kind of weed. I feel proud as a midwife delivering octuplets. I first saw the baby hostas from a standing position, but it was not until I got down on all fours that I saw the upright arch of their leaves and their distinct veining and thought they had a good chance of being something other than plantain. I make a mental note to take a closer look more often.

I make a mental note to wear knee pads too. Not that I don't like the feel of cool soil on my skin, but the hosta project reminds me that a gardener needs to respect her own life as much as the lives of the plants. I need to be attentive to cuts and thorns, to tendonitis, and especially to my knees. If I ever lose the ability to get down on my knees, I will miss things like the baby hostas, not to mention a good share of my garden tasks.

I am on my knees weeding some red monarda I planted (also from my sister) on the day a hummingbird comes right at me in search of nectar. I panic, certain he is lining up his long, pointy beak with the black pupil of my right eye. He flaps furiously in front of me for a couple of seconds before reversing direction and taking off.

Once the danger passes, I savor the thrill of looking this amazing creature in the eye, or at least the face (his eye having been too small). I sense our tacit agreement to stagger our visits to the monarda patch so as not to get in each other's way.

Making myself scarce in the garden, I see firsthand how much interaction there is between flowers and birds. They are, except if garden chemicals are present, naturally suited to each other. The well-tended soil is home to worms, providing a welcome feast, especially when nestlings need food. Even a hose left untended is cause for celebration to a bird and he invites the whole neighborhood. And then there are the seeds. Birds eat them, and scatter them. New flowers grow in unlikely places.

One seed dropped by a bird, or the wind, results in a six-foot sunflower in my garden. I walk out just after sunrise one morning to see a wren fly toward it. He perches on the stem of one of the dinner-plate-sized leaves. In front of him, between the two of us, hangs another leaf. All of this is backlit by the sun so the wren is silhouetted on the leaf as he sings his morning song.

I am only six or eight feet away. I can see his throat vibrate with the power of those beautiful notes. He doesn't see me because the leaf is between us. He seems to sing his joy of the new day, and maybe of his pleasure in the beauty of the garden. He sings what I feel but do not express. I hang a wren house on a shepherd's hook in the garden after that, hoping to see that same sight again, but I don't. I am thankful to have seen it once.

One morning, a few weeks later, while I am down on hands and knees, I begin to hear a squeaking I cannot identify. At first I think the sound is coming from within one of the clumps of peonies or somewhere at ground level. I know snakes don't make sounds like that, but still I tense up a little, sure some predator like a ferocious chipmunk must be nearby. Then I look up.

There, on the hook above me, the wren house is shaking back and forth, having its own little earthquake. When I go over to check it out, I can tell the squeaking is coming from inside. Before I get too close, the wren mother comes out on the perch to warn me off. I tell her I am a mother too, and so I understand her fierce squawking. I affirm it. Leaving my tools behind, I head back to the house. There are times, like this one, when a closer look tells us to go away.

Still, if I did not get down on my knees for a closer look at the world, I would miss not only the weeds that need pulling, but also the knowledge that I share the garden with chirping wrens. I would miss the different kinds of beauty Lake Superior offers and I would miss the hummingbird asserting his rights. I would miss tiny hostas, or something very much like hostas, and the gift of imagining them as huge specimens one day.

Truly, a thing that brings me to my knees is not necessarily a bad thing. Unless it is quack.

Did you ever wonder if hostas and plantains are in the same family since they look so much alike? Once hostas were called "Plantain Lilies," and so it's clear that people have linked them for some time. Now, however, they are classified in two different families. Hostas are classified as Agavaceae (which means they are more closely related to plants like the agave), while plantains are classified under Plantaginaceae. Whew! No more guilt about getting rid of plantain.

# 11

# When Only Rebar Will Do

Every gardener probably holds a soft spot, even if only a small one, for plants that offer to help out in the garden for free. Volunteers. They start out small. Some never manage to thrive. Some get out of hand. No matter what their other characteristics, however, they all seem to have one thing in common: They sprout up in places we don't want them. Some say that a weed is just a flower in the wrong place. I do not always believe this. I believe that quack is a weed and it has no place. Volunteers are another matter.

Earlier in the summer I had found tomatoes volunteering among the roses and decided to let them grow, even though I wondered just what they were doing among the flowers. Now I consider their odd placement every time I look at them, trying to unravel the mystery of what came before me in this place. I suspect I missed my calling as an archaeologist.

The volunteer tomatoes reward me in late summer, all by chance, with small, pear-shaped, yellow fruit completely different from any I ever grew before, and very tasty. So much of gardening is about chance, I'm discovering: the chance of hot weather that makes the yellow tomatoes thrive versus the cool temps that might have halted their germination from last year's seeds, the chance of too much rain, or too little, the chance of hungry deer or rabbits passing by or not, the chance I will be gone the week the beans should be picked, the chance I will actually plant something in its optimum location with regard to sun, height, width, or color on the first try. I am not only *not* in command of quack, but increasingly, I realize, not in control of much else in the garden either.

Both chance and planning, I realize, have gone into the creation of the many varieties that exist. Take tomatoes, for example. Hybridization has created the Better Boy and Early Girl varieties, but what we now call heirloom tomatoes probably owe their existence, in large part, to chance mutations. The seeds of these new varieties were saved by patient gardeners who wanted to get that same strain the next year. Over time, many varieties of the same species evolve by self-seeding too—in case one is accidentally eradicated, others will carry on.

As Kenny Ausubel says in his book, *Seeds of Change,* "Variety is not only the spice of life, but the very staff of life. Diversity is nature's fail-safe mechanism against extinction. It provides the vast genetic pool of accumulated experiences and characteristics from which change can originate." (The *Seeds of Change* catalogue offers over sixty-five varieties of tomatoes alone, about one-third of those actually grown in field trials. Wow. Who knew?)

So, all of my volunteers have a purpose, but they aren't telling me about it. And unless I live to be a hundred years old, I may never see the subtle change from yellow to orange in this particular tomato, but if that happens, it is because there is a historical reason for it in nature.

The tomatoes, of course, are not the only volunteers in the garden. Sunflowers also came up here and there in late spring. If one has ever had sunflowers in the garden, even once, birds and squirrels will see to it they pretty much continue to show up forever. Obviously, the previous gardeners here had sunflowers. Now I have them too.

In the early summer I begin to transplant volunteers, making them not really volunteers at all, I suppose. Conscripts? Some I transplant before they are strong enough. They wilt over into pathetic little mounds, which tells me I should have

waited until the seedlings were bigger and stronger. By the time others are ready, we have come to the scorching summer days whose temperatures rival those of Phoenix or Death Valley. Thus, most of my transplants do not survive the move. I hope, desperately, that these are not some rare mutative species.

Those that do survive have a long period of transplant shock during which they mope and do not grow. And, in addition to these drawbacks, they do not necessarily look any better, or fit in any better than they did in the place *they* had chosen for their new address. So much for going to all of this extra work.

When, at last, some transplants take off for the sun, I assume they will take care of themselves and I go on to other tasks. After all, the five sunflowers I did *not* move are growing along in glorious fashion, tall, straight, and quite beautiful. They rise up like periscopes out of the sea of pink and white and blue that I have been struggling to maintain. They adhere to no order whatsoever, but they are showy and I am pleased with them. The transplants, on the other hand, decide to take care of themselves by growing at odd angles, not at all the direction I think they should be going.

When a mid-summer thunderstorm pounds the garden, laying the sunflowers on their sides, I feel sorry for them. The cosmos I planted in the vegetable garden are flattened too. The soil is so wet I cannot get in the garden to straighten things up for three or four days. The reclining flowers, of course, do not wait for me. They immediately begin growing skyward from their prone position because they are programmed to grow straight up, whatever their starting point.

I don't catch on to this at first. I come to the garden the two mornings after the rain, hoping to see that the sunflowers have somehow sprung back to their original upright position. Each morning I'm disappointed. I ignore the new growth now at right angles to the rest of the stem. When I look at them a few days later, the sunflowers have grown another foot and have L-shaped stems. These plants need staking, no matter how much soil compaction occurs in the still-soaked garden. I race to the scrap lumber pile in the garage for materials.

We brought lots of one-by-one-inch oak pieces with us from the other house (amusing our movers no end) but these seem intended for some higher purpose. I find some pine scraps too, but I can tell right away that none of them will ever hold up a sunflower. Metal fence posts seem like overkill, and, besides, I can only find two of them. I look to the oak pieces again. My current purpose elevates itself. I cut the oak into three-foot lengths and grab a ball of twine.

Staking an already crooked plant is not a gratifying exercise. I consider never allowing cosmos in my garden again, but back off and satisfy myself with a vow to stake earlier next year, because cosmos are the darlings of my old fashioned bouquets. Next year they will likely self-seed, volunteer, and cost nothing but time. I have to do what I can for them.

The ground is still deeply saturated from the heavy rains accompanying the windstorm that caused my problems in the first place, and I can feel the oak pieces tipping from the weight of the plants. I pound the stakes in deeper, which makes them shorter, and less effective.

The next morning, the plants view the world from a gently reclining position once again. Perhaps oak is not quite as sturdy as I thought it was when I watched the red oaks hold their leaves last winter? I allow that it probably is and that I am not using the stakes properly. I make a mental note to cut longer pieces next time, but I can already tell that will not be enough for the sunflowers.

Like so many things in the garden, success in staking my sunflowers finally owes itself to my mother-in-law, giver of so many perennials and of so much good advice. She has saved rebar fencing material since the day, ten years ago, when she and my father-in-law left their farm. At the first word of my staking trials, she gives me a dozen three-foot posts with u-shaped legs at the bottom to help hold them in place. They are rusted to a warm bronze that will be unobtrusive in the garden. As I pound them in, I can tell they will not move. The soil is drier by this time, and the posts' two legs are better than one.

As I place each rebar wonder, I envision sunflowers standing tall during the winter, even if their stalks have a couple of bends in them. They will be picked clean of their seeds by cardinals and nuthatches and blue jays. I know I will see snow sculpt the stalks into works of garden art. In the spring, I will pull the sunflowers up, even though they are still fibrous and strong and would no doubt be glad to go on volunteering throughout the summer too. New volunteers will come along to take their place.

A friend of mine, chuckling over the rebar solution and the odd placement of sunflowers in my garden, notes her surprise that other plants are doing so well around them. Sunflowers, she tells me, can be toxic to other plants. Great, I think, a toxic volunteer. What's next? Exploding atomic sunflowers? I envision my garden the next year totally devoid of all of the perennials that I have been so carefully tending. My friend goes on to say that sunflowers interact unfavorably, primarily with fruit and vegetable crops. I breathe a sigh of relief. I do not plan on having many fruits or vegetables next year—I'm sticking with flowers. I later learn that it's the hulls of the seeds that have a toxic effect, not necessarily the plants themselves. Again, relief.

Rabbits have destroyed my beets, carrots, and lettuce this year. Only the pole beans on the little trellis have been spared. Next year I will not offer creatures such a buffet. I am already thinking about what new perennials to plant in the teardrop garden.

Staking these self-seeding annuals strikes me, suddenly, as little more than promoting disorder not only in this year's garden, but also in next year's. Why would I do such a thing? Perhaps because I can see that while having an orderly garden is a wonderful thing, it's just not a wonderful thing for me.

I suspect I may be alone in this kind of approach when I look at the orderly gardens of friends and family, until I learn from a neighbor that her secret to the beautiful color palette in her garden is to buy packets of annual flower seeds and just throw them out among her perennials. Whatever comes up in a given spot is allowed to have its life. It provides surprises, and proves that, in nature, all colors work together.

Nature seems to like it both ways: perfect order in the arrangement of petals on a rose, and no semblance of order whatsoever in the ways volunteer plants are seeded. I decide that if it's good enough for nature, it's good enough for me, and I lose some of my anxiety over the garden. There is beauty in human-inspired order, but there is also beauty in natural disorder. In the world of volunteers, I learn to love observing what the plants can do on their own, without any gardener's hand. I learn that they do very well without me, and probably in spite of me.

I try to be helpful to volunteers where I can, but I remain in denial about the volunteer quack in the irises, peonies, daylilies, and Siberians. I'm sick of even the minimal amount of cosmetic weeding I've been doing, tired of wearing a wrist brace for my tendonitis, and yet I can't quite bring myself to do away with all of the flowers in the four problem rows.

Getting rid of flowers just to get rid of quack? Wouldn't that set biodiversity into a tailspin? Problems imply solutions. I find myself wishing for a magic product to solve my problems with quack, but even my mother-in-law can't come up with that. The day of reckoning lies ahead. I just don't know when.

Volunteer sunflowers, unlike the problem rows, have taught me much about how and when and whether to transplant, about how to get a natural look in the garden, and about the different ways plants can grow. These sunflowers, taller than I am, remind me I have a place in this world, but not necessarily the main place. Plants, I'm coming to understand, are infinitely more complex than I've previously imagined. If they ever take over the earth, I, for one, want to be on the good side of them.

Bring on the volunteers.

Did you ever wonder how to be a better staker (even beyond rebar)? I can offer you only one bit of advice: start early. When you plant your dahlia bulbs in May, set a stake (or two or three) in next to them and deep enough so that it won't be tipped over when the dahlias get heavy with blooms. When peonies are just beet-red fingers poking out of the ground, get those peony cages in place. I admit, I don't have cages for all of my peonies—but someday I hope to because I know the peonies will thank me. Stakes are your promise to the plants that you have faith in what they will become. They need that kind of support as much as we do. Plants are just like children: they will reward you for the time you invest in them.

# 12

# What's in a Name?

Logs and rocks lurking beneath the surface of the water that raise havoc with hulls and outboard motors are called *deadheads*, presumably because they can stop you dead and because the word "head" rhymes conveniently with "dead." *Deadheads* are people who follow the band "The Grateful Dead." A *deadhead* is a person who goes to the movies or rides a bus or plane using a free ticket. *Deadheading* means making a trip with no passengers, such as when an airliner flies a load of tourists from Minnesota to Florida in the winter and returns empty, then picks up another load and repeats the process. These are all *deadheading*. They are not what I do in the garden as June turns into July.

The seventy-eight bushes full of faded roses—no, now eighty-three (I found five more when I cleaned out weeds in the spring)—need my immediate attention, needed it a week or two back if I'm to be honest. I seem to have this built-in delay mechanism that makes me chronically late for tasks so that every task can be more difficult than it should be. I make a mental note to try to be more punctual in the future, although I don't note how much more.

Consulting one of the books on roses I'd purchased at the auction just a year earlier,

when the gardens were going to be just a small bit of decoration for the house, I read that roses need to be deadheaded if you want them to bloom again. And varieties that only bloom once should not be deadheaded. How am I to know which is which? Reading on, I find that, if not deadheaded, some roses will begin to form hips too early, which will sap their energy so much that they can die out over winter. I know I don't want that to happen.

As I consider where and how to begin deadheading, I decide that few things in the garden are as ill-named as this process. *Deadheading* always makes it sound as though the plants are dead, when of course they are very much alive and only looking for a chance to start over. It also makes them sound like they are stupid, when, of course, they are so wise about their own rhythms that they know when and how to bloom completely without our interference. True, the spent blooms are dead looking, but the appearance does not fully indicate the reality.

Disposing of the spent blooms is a kind of garden housekeeping, a way of making things look nice, the way we might dust off a coffee table or wash a window. Why not call it gardenkeeping? Not specific enough, no doubt—could mean weeding, could mean mulching, could mean staking, could mean spraying, and could even mean planting. (Could mean eradicating quack...)

Books try to be specific about things when they tell people what needs to be done in the garden, and deadheading is pretty specific. Just not very appealing. When I come across the word "disbudding" in a British publication, I think I may have hit on something better, but when I read on I find that this means "removing side buds … [which] allows the stronger terminal bud to develop to its maximum size". Great. Another thing I don't know how to do. I need to know how and whether to take off spent rose blooms. Now.

Ortho's *All About Roses*, a thin paperback, bears a sticker that says "American Rose Society Endorsement." Good enough for me. It tells me to make an angle cut just above the last five-leaf cluster below the faded bloom. This seems simple enough.

Armed with newly purchased pruning shears, I go to the garden early in the morning, planning to complete the task before coffee break. Let's see: was it just above or just below the five leaves? I go back to the house, get the book, and take it with me to the garden.

I'm wearing my new leather garden gloves, recommended by the books, but their seams irritate my fingers as I push my wheelbarrow out to the rose garden. The gloves' stiff hide is not at all suited for the fine muscle work of clipping off tiny rose stems, so I take them off. After the first stab from the pink Grootendorst rose's thorns, I put them back on again.

Just as the book told me, below each bloom I find first a single leaf or two, then perhaps three leaves on a stem, and finally the five together. Textbook. I snip away, dropping faded blooms into the wheelbarrow as the sun climbs. One bush down, eighty-two to go. Bush number two has five leaves directly below the bloom. No singles. Hmmm. I cut above them and also prune away a few pieces of deadwood that I missed in my spring pruning.

The wheelbarrow is beginning to fill and the sun is climbing higher. I go on to bushes three and four where I cut away whole clumps of blooms before I hit five leaves on a stem. All of the blooms are spent, and so this seems fine. But also odd. Aren't they all rose bushes? Shouldn't they all grow in the same manner?

I dump the wheelbarrow and go on to the next bushes, perspiration now beginning to stream down under the sweat band on my topee. I feel a little weak at the thought of another seventy-plus roses to go, then comfort myself with the thought that some of them, at least, are miniatures. Some only have a bloom or two. It is only the big shrub roses that have so many. My leather gloves are keeping my hands safe, but my forearms are scratched and bleeding. I make a note to wear long sleeves, no matter how hot the day, before I ever do this again. Like tomorrow.

It takes me three days to completely clean up the roses, and then I realize that other plants also need attention. I have planted a clump of shasta daisies in an empty spot in one of the rose beds. In their eagerness to please, they have reached three feet tall or more, and have pretty much overpowered everything planted within two feet of them. Cutting away the now brown daisies will give the plants patiently waiting in their shadow a chance to show their faces to the world.

The daisies, of course, are not ready to give up. When my pruning shears trace their way down the daisy stalk to find a place to cut near the bottom, they find that the next crop is already sprouting and ready to take off. I take a deep breath. More work for me, I realize, but at the same time I see the daisies telling me that it all has a purpose, which, apparently, is not just renewed growth but also to make me feel totally inadequate. When I look over my shoulder, I see that all of the irises and peonies should have been deadheaded long ago too.

I look up from one clump of daisies to see the row of shrub roses neatly pruned, cleaned up like bachelors ready for a Saturday night date. Satisfaction floods me. Who could imagine that cutting things back could make them look better? Like new again? An old adage for writers says that what you take out is just as important as what you leave in—and so it is with plants. Maybe even more so.

So, maybe it would be good to take out the term "deadheading" and change it to . . . to what? Freshening? Doesn't "I'm going out to freshen up the roses" sound a lot more inviting than "I'm going out to deadhead the roses"? Freshening. I like the sound of the word. I picture the roses freshening themselves up with perfume as they get ready to go out for the evening. I see them swirl their beautiful gowns. I deny their thorns in all of this.

After I finish the roses in the main garden, I work on the garden near the front entrance to the house, the front dooryard garden. It was a white garden before we came, but I didn't know it at the time. This is the garden where I had hurriedly planted the irises I brought with me from the other house right after we moved in, before I knew that this place has more irises than one person can actually manage. I also stuck in some other perennials I brought with me, barely getting their roots under the soil and using no plan whatsoever. It is no longer a white garden, because queen of the prairie, a blue delphinium, and a yellow lily are planted there. Now it is just another garden. I realize my mistake at this point, but am not sure I want to move all of these things when I have another whole bed of quack/irises/peonies to cope with, and so I try to freshen this area, cutting away the pink, blue and yellow blooms, so that the Iceberg roses and white lilies can commune in peace along with a moss-covered tree stump.

The stump seems a little out of place, even at the edge of the woods where the garden lies. It seems a little rustic amid the white laciness of the other flowers. I am tempted to just pull it up with my hands because it is well decayed and only the moss is holding it together, but when my hands touch it, something stops me. "Keep it all as natural as you can," I remember my gardener sister telling me when she first visited the place.

The moss is soft and resilient. As I bend toward it, I see each little stem and fringe of green. Are they stems and flowers? How, exactly, does moss grow? Suddenly the stump isn't too rustic for the garden at all, but is instead like a velvet backdrop in a jewelry store. No garden is "just" a garden, no matter what its color scheme.

It occurs to me that my tendency toward the positive, toward freshening versus deadheading, may be just another way of avoiding even the hint of talking about death, but I don't think so. As I work among them, I see that flowers exemplify the power of beauty, the resonance of repetition and the promise of new life. They have their purpose and I do not want to saddle it with nomenclature like deadheading that dismisses any part of their lives as unimportant, stupid, or less than wholesome. I wonder what they would like to call me? Perhaps I can rise in their estimation if I promise to keep freshening them, because I can see that they like it.

Unfreshened, most plants will still find a way to bloom when they are supposed to, through the scattering of their seeds or the ability of their roots to cling to life despite the perils of climate and human carelessness with shears, hoe, or herbicide. At the beginning of that first day in the roses, I saw deadheading as a task. A huge task. The more I do it, the more I realize that it is something I do for myself as much as for the plant. It's a way of pleasing my own eyes and spirit. Besides, I find relaxation in the challenge of finding just the right place to make my cut, in cutting at the right angle, and in finding the right way to avoid thorns (is there such a thing?).

The freshened plant focuses its energy either on its roots (so that it can send up new shoots from the bottom or just become a stronger, bigger plant for the next season) or on re-blooming... and re-blooming. Some plants will continue blooming until the season changes and they can bloom no more. Freshening to enable such a blind passion for life is not a burden, but a gift, one I am thankful to have received.

As I try to learn more about how better to care for the roses, it is clear that different kinds of roses require different kinds of care, and that if I can identify the different types I have, I can probably find their care information in one of the books I have.

In my early spring weeding around the bases of the shrub roses, I uncovered a small plastic tag with some faded lettering on it, the kind of thing that comes with plants bought at a greenhouse, so now I go back to the garden and take another look.

Sure enough, there they are, buried under the soil—tags on all of the shrub roses. Red Grootendorst, Roseraie de la Hay, Magnifica, Jens Munk, Hansa, Pink Grootendorst, Sarah Van Fleet (I can't quite read this one and it bothers me—I want to know more about her), Glauca Rosa Rubiflora, David A. Austin Heritage English Rose, Charleese de Mills. I record them all in the garden journal I'm starting, and make a note to try to find the names of all of the other roses too.

Graham Stuart Thomas's *Shrub Roses of Today* is my go-to source on how to care for the plants I've now connected with a name. Thomas surprises me by singing the praises of the single rose, the one with only five petals, the one that blooms only once a year. He must be nuts, I think. But as I read on, I find I agree with him: while other, newer rose varieties may have more petals, deeper color, or fewer thorns, there is something about the single, wild rose, the one beloved of everyone from ancient Greeks to English kings to American pioneers, which connects us to the earth with just a breath of its scent. Thomas probably owned hundreds of varieties of beautiful roses, yet he kept going back to the beauty of the single rose—his gold standard.

I look at the one shrub rose bush I have not unearthed a tag for. My sister told me it was probably a variety called Nearly Wild. It has the most vicious thorns of all the roses in the gardens. It grows to over ten feet and then arches over so that it can hook me by the back every time I walk or mow under it. It has bloomed once with small pink flowers. Each may have had five petals, I really didn't take time to notice, and already it is forming scads of hips. Hmmm. This, too, has a place in the garden. Even if it should be called "Killer." And best of all, I've now learned it's one of only two shrubs in my garden that does not require freshening. And certainly not deadheading.

Did you ever wonder just how many varieties of roses are in the world? A quick Internet search told me there are 6,500—a nice, pat answer I didn't believe. I searched further. It turns out that the word "variety" can mean different things. Some may be talking about species, some about cultivars. Because roses are constantly being hybridized and improved, maybe we would be safest in just saying there are thousands of kinds of roses, one for every temperament. We could spend a lifetime getting to know them all—and wouldn't that be a beautiful pursuit?

# 13

# Of Barns and Buicks

E ver since we moved in last October, I have been placing all my potato peelings, coffee grounds, and other organic material into a brown plastic composter that came to us, half-full, with the house. It sits about ten feet from the garage, convenient but not the most beautiful thing in the world. Now it is mid-summer, and as the temperature begins to approach ninety-degrees, the composter is also not the sweetest smelling part of my gardening operation. I go to the library for a book on composting to find out what I'm doing wrong. The answer: pretty much everything.

"Layer green and brown," the book says. It doesn't say anything about orange and yellow or red. "Grinding all of your compostable kitchen waste", it says, "will speed up the composting process". Grinding? I raise my eyebrows as I read this. I have my limits, and the mere idea of how much work this would entail is almost too much for me. I may not know much about composting, but I know I'm not grinding. Period. I make a mental note to never, never, never grind compost.

"Turn the compost pile weekly," the book says. Weekly? Oh, sure. I don't want to be out in the garden picking roses—no, I'd rather be turning my compost pile. The person who wrote the book obviously doesn't have roses, or quack in his iris bed.

When I think of compost, I think of a former neighbor, an eighty-five-year-old retired farmer. On the first warm day of the spring, he never failed to take two five-gallon plastic pails from his garage, put them into the trunk of his Buick LeSabre, and drive to the livestock auction barn. He would fill the pails with cow manure from a big pile in the corner of the feedlot, bring them home, and dig the contents into the row of hybrid tea roses he had planted under the dining room windows right after he and his wife moved to town.

Some years later, when his wife was moved to the local nursing home, he took her a beautiful rose every day during the summer and well into fall. Often he brought them over for me to see first, causing one of my early bouts of garden envy.

Laying the compost book aside, I set off to check out the three other compost bins I've noticed lurking in the woods. These bins are made of a green, plastic-coated wire and hold about a cubic yard when full. Unfortunately, they sit too far away from the gardens to be very useful. On the plus side, they do not smell. From a distance they appear to be almost empty, but I suspect there may be compost hiding at the bottom.

After fighting my way through some underbrush, I excavate what I can into my wheelbarrow from bin number one, where six inches of dark, chunky material covers the bottom. As I dig, I hear the voice from the composting book say that "all compost should be screened before being transferred to the garden". I decide to skip that step so that I can clean out the bins and move them to more convenient locations.

The take from the first bin does not fill my wheel barrow, yet I am sweating from my efforts. All but the top three or four inches of material has been filled with web-like tree roots impossible to penetrate with the shovel. I recall that the composting book has repeatedly referred to compost as "black gold" and tell myself that I don't need *a lot* of gold to have a treasure. Just an ounce will do. Still, somehow, I doubt that all of these tree roots have any real value, except to the tree from which they are now parted.

When I consider where to bury my treasure, I decide on a strip of ground near the shrub roses where the previous owners presumably had a few vegetables planted among the three miniature rose bushes, because this is where the yellow tomatoes are thriving. This plot has been largely ignored while I've been carving out the new teardrop garden, and I decide it's now time to reward it for its patience. I dump my wheel barrow with significantly less confidence than a Forty-Niner taking his buckskin bag of gold dust to the assayer's office.

I begin to work the soil, tossing out weeds and suspicious-looking roots, and as I do I notice evidence of eggshells, and walnut shells, and snail shells. Snail shells? Up until this point I have never thought of snails living anywhere other than near a lake or river. Now I find that snails are inordinately fond of woodlands too. And they do not know my garden is not part of their woodland, so they graze at will. Their cousins, the slugs, also feel they can dine wherever they like. I make a mental note to check out another book, this one on the control of gastropods.

I know I should rake off the other chunks of not-quite-composted material, because they'll never turn to black gold lying there on top of the ground, at least not in time to do these plants any good. Their destination should be the compost bin, again, where time and temperature can work their miracles, but I'm lazy and leave them, hoping for the miracle that no one will notice them.

The miracle of the whole thing, though, seems to be that rotting vegetable peelings are actually a growth activity and not a death activity, despite the smell that might indicate the contrary. It makes me just a tad nervous to realize how closely the two concepts are related, but I let it go. I will do the best I can to spin straw into gold. But I still don't think I will get the compost turned every week. I'm just not that good.

As I work in the remaining compost, I see traces of newspaper with which the previous owners mulched. One half-sheet of the *Rochester Post-Bulletin* lies crisp, but intact, under a layer of dust. The composting book tells me that "newspapers make a good weed barrier. Six or seven pages thick will do, and later they just self-compost." Obviously the other pages of the *Post-Bulletin* have done just that, because weeds are thriving there among the phlox, coneflowers, blue bells and Russian sage I have brought with me and planted in this one open bed.

Canadian thistles large enough to feed a family of four sprout up every few inches, accompanied by weeds I can't identify. The dried, curled-up newspaper segment looks like a vagrant in need of a bath. I chop it into pieces and bury it. When the plot looks as good as I can make it, I stand back to admire the three-by-twenty-foot expanse of black earth and healthy green plants. Here and there bits of newsprint stand like tiny mutineers. I turn my back on them without so much as a word, hoping for a heavy rain.

Then I look to the shade garden, which I have not touched since early spring. No black earth there. Weeds tower over the hostas. I must be doing something wrong *besides* my faulty composting, I tell myself. The only good news is that the weeds are not quack. In fact, most are wildflowers, namely wild geraniums. (Flowers in the wrong place?) The irregular planting pattern here makes landscape fabric impractical—there are no rows. Maybe the only inexpensive way to get control here is to use newspaper mulch (lots of it!) the way the previous owners did, even if it encourages some vagrancy. But what should I use to cover the newspaper with so that it can't be seen and doesn't all blow away in the first thunderstorm?

I recall seeing a pile of decaying leaves up behind a small shed. I had been planning just to let them compost away out of my sight via benign neglect, but now I realize I can hasten the process by making use of them over the newspapers. Still honing my shifting skills with the Ford, I manage to haul a load of the brown leaves from *up* by the brush pile to *down* beside the shade garden without killing the engine once.

After removing as many weeds as I can, I lay out a month's supply of the *Minneapolis Star Tribune* on the ground, taking off my gloves occasionally to tear out a good recipe or an editorial I want to mull over, along with other parts of the papers I missed during my weeks of outdoor chores. Soon the hostas are surrounded with stories. There is so much to love in the daily paper.

Next, using a five-gallon pail to scoop up leaves, I cover the newsprint with damp, musty promise four inches deep. An hour later, I have depleted the truck full of leaves as well as the stack of papers that would otherwise have gone to recycling. There is just one problem: I have still not quite covered the shade garden. As I rev up the truck to haul another load, a small stash of saved newsprint strips grows limp on the dewy grass of late morning.

With the shade garden fully mulched, I fold the saved recipes and unread articles into a small bundle and stuff it in my shirt pocket, then return to my composting campaign, moving on to bin number two. It is nestled in some hazelnut brush on the far side of the driveway. In the nine months we have lived at the house I have never actually walked up to it.

When I do, I find no compost to load. Instead, I see only the remains of four standard roses—topiaries grown in large pots. My heart begins to beat in rapid runs. Garden envy, even this imagined variety, once again turns me green and almost induces me to set these back in some soil to see if they will grow, but I know that after they have spent a winter with their roots exposed to sub-zero temps they have no life left in them. And they probably had no life in them when someone tossed them out into the compost bin, or near it, but, of course, I wonder about this. Did someone mistake dormancy for death?

I pick them up and look them over for signs of life, but they're brittle and on their way to compost right there in the woods no matter how much I want them. I tell myself not to feel cheated they're gone, but to instead remember how many beautiful roses and other plants I have already inherited with this property. But part of me still longs for what has been lost, and my green feet are a little slower as they plod to bin three.

It, too, is empty. Its black, plastic bottom liner is torn and looking like the worst kind of litter. Eight twelve-inch bisque chimney flues, each one about thirty inches high, have been tossed in next to it helter-skelter. I have been looking at these creatures ever since we moved to the house, wondering how to get them out of sight. I lift the end of one, scrape off the soil accumulated on its bottom side, and decide it may have possibilities. I just don't know what they are.

There is nothing to do at this point but go back to the brown plastic compost bin and move it as far from the house as possible. When I lift the lid, flies swarm out as though even they can't stand the stench. The putrid mass below has sunk to about half the height of the bin, and I realize it is composting, despite my failures to provide the right ingredients.

I attempt to open the little sliding door on the bottom where I can, presumably, scoop out black gold while the layers above it turn from orange and green to black, but the door won't slide. Lifting up the whole bin doesn't work either, since the plastic frame has settled nicely down into the soil. Again I excavate. Then I pry. Finally one side breaks loose, then another. I lift up the bin, and a pile of rotting, oozing, stinking gunk slides toward my feet. The only salvation is that no rodent or snake slides out with it.

I grab my shovel again and load the mess into the wheel barrow. Never in my life would I have believed that there could be anything more repellent than shoveling manure, but I decide that decaying veggies and fruits may actually be worse. Nevertheless, I get the mucky mess out of there and distribute it among the other three bins, all of which I have now sited more conveniently to the gardens, at a good distance from the house. I remember that there are a few leaves in the pile I drew from to cover the newspapers, so I follow up with a layer of brown—just like the book said.

The green layer needed next is delivered to me, quite without my wanting it, when after ten days of, what seems like, endless rain we are forced to rake the grass clippings off of the lawn after mowing. Small haystacks cover the lawn and the family unites to load them into the garden cart and dump them onto the compost piles. I can immediately see that I now have too much green, but I don't care. I just want the grass OFF THE LAWN.

A couple of days later, I decide to test the theory about turning the pile and stick a fork into one of the heaps of grass. To my surprise, it's actually hot. Ever since I first heard about a barn burning because it had been filled with wet hay, I had tried to figure out how that could have even been possible. I mean, wouldn't it have to be dry hay? Dry as the proverbial tinder? I realize now how such a fire can be possible: Decaying matter actually gives off energy, along with odor, in the form of heat.

I immediately envision the compost bin igniting, the fire spreading to the house, and other worst case scenarios. I get hold of my imagination before I feel forced to dig all the way to the bottom of the compost pile where the rotting gunk would be encountered again. I'm just not doing it. Not even for black gold. Not even if it makes roses grow with five hundred petals each.

When the weather clears and the gardens dry out enough for me to set foot in them again, I check out the little plot where I added the compost. The soil is draining nicely. It does not smell. Weeds are still there, but they pull easily. The soil still shows bits of egg shells, but they are not unsightly, and the newspaper mutineers have mostly surrendered. I admit that the composting book may have some merits after all.

I admit, too, that my old neighbor using his otherwise pristine Buick to haul pails of cow manure has taught me something about composting that goes well beyond the book. The neighbor wasn't just enriching the soil. He wasn't just growing prize-winning, quality roses. He was growing love. His face beamed not with pride at his gardening ability when he showed me his roses, but with the gift he was able to give the wife who no longer knew even what decade she was living in. She was still able to see and smell the beauty of each new rose. She often told him that he made her feel like a young bride again. To grow and give one such rose, I realize, is a goal worthy of any gardener. If we enrich the soil of our lives, we will grow ourselves roses.

In the shade garden, the leaf mulch has settled comfortably over the *Star Tribune*. It looks neat and orderly, even though part of an editorial appears here and there. I notice tell-tale holes on some of the hosta leaves, causing me to imagine armies of slugs hiding under the papers, possibly working the crossword puzzles I have not had time to do, and it occurs to me that I should rip all of the papers out of there—but if I do, the weeds will be back. Using the newspaper weed barrier has helped me get this garden under control, and keep it within my self-imposed limits. I will have to make a choice: a few holes in the hostas or weeds I may never be able to get under control.

I apologize to the hostas and walk back to the house, making a mental note to buy a six-pack of beer the next time I go to town. One can for the slugs.

> Did you ever wonder what to do with all of those rose petals? I once made rose petal jelly, which was sweet but not all that flavorful. I have since read that the petals used must be from the most heavily scented roses (I probably did not do this). The recipe I used has long since escaped me, but now an Internet search turns up several of them (also a soup with chilled pears—who knew?) Cooks.com recommends using Hansen rose petals, which I hope are the same as those on my Hansen Hedge Roses. If so, I have them in abundance and will try again. Serving rose petal jelly is an elegant delight that will impress your friends and sweeten up your enemies. Worth a try, eh?

# 14

# A
# Slippery
# Slope

Fighting my mental battle with quack, I wonder more and more about the intentions of the gardeners who planted the four long rows of irises and their compatriots. Why did they leave such wide grassy strips between them? Did they intend to drive a lawn tractor through them (as I would if the space were only a little wider)? Had they wanted the perennials to spread and fill up that space but the grass filled it instead? Were they trying to give it an English garden look with elegant grass paths, but then the grass got away from them?

My life crosses, right there on those paths, with the gardeners who cared for this space before me. I ask, almost daily, for their input and each day they seem to be saying that the only way to conquer quack is to get rid of the grass strips between the perennials. But they do not say how. Really? The idea of getting rid of long grass strips keeps popping up—just the way the quack grass does.

So, that's it then. I'm going to pursue a low-maintenance plan for the hundreds of irises; the peonies, more than twenty clumps; daylilies, mounds that spill in all directions like water from a fountain; and the stately Siberian irises, which, now in August, wear their dried seed pods like scepters.

I sense it is a watershed decision, except I don't yet know in what sense. I only know that getting rid of the grass and then tilling the former strips weekly is going to be a lot easier than trying to pull out the quack. After all, it's basically what I do in the vegetable garden and it seems to work.

Out come the clear plastic sheets that I have been using as drop cloths for painting in the house. I spread them on the grass. Two weeks will kill off the grass, I have read. Since I don't have enough plastic to do the whole area at once, I begin with half of one row. I secure the plastic with bricks, boards, and anything else I can find. This whole suffocation process seems heartless, and the plastic makes the lawn look littered, but I decide to go with it for the greater good of the flowers.

Every day I watch it. After six days, the grass begins to yellow. Then, the plastic comes loose in a few places and green springs up anew within hours. I batten down the proverbial hatches again and wait. Six days. Yellowing. Green. After two weeks, I have spots of brown and spots of yellow and spots of green. Well, a garden is for color, after all.

Clearly (no pun intended) this plastic is not working quite as well as promised. There is nothing to do but get out my Mantis rototiller, which will turn the whole thing brown in no time. By now I know from my reading that tilling will actually encourage quack roots by cutting them into tiny pieces, each of which can then root, yet this seems like my only recourse. In deep denial, I till.

I keep tilling, every couple of weeks, thinking I'm not only eradicating quack but also doing much good, both aesthetically and qualitatively for the soil. Then I read that tilling too deeply brings up new weed seeds that have lain dormant and would have continued to lie dormant if I had not disturbed them. As I see new leaf patterns develop between tillings, I realize this is probably true.

Thanks to my tilling, I not only have quack but wild asters and pigweed and a quick-multiplying little number with tongue-shaped leaves I wish I had never met. In addition, by breaking up the soil into such tiny particles as it does, I learn that tilling also contributes to compacting. *Great.*

I realize I cannot keep tilling like this forever. It takes more time than I thought it would, but worse, the loose soil erodes in heavy rains, which we are having almost weekly this summer. The long S-shaped rows of perennials run down a twenty-five degree slope, and finally I realize that my predecessors probably planted the grass between them in order to keep all of the topsoil from washing away. I must have heard them wrong.

This summer, on every visit to a garden center I look at landscape fabric and pass it by: *too expensive, not right for me.* Now I realize landscape fabric and wood mulch are my only hope of saving the soil before the next rain. Still unwilling to spring for the landscape fabric, I bring out a stash of black plastic purchased at the garage sale where we bought the pickup, but I throw thoughts of cost to the wind as I rush to town for ten bags of cedar mulch. There may be quack among the plants, but the space between the rows is going to look beautiful, I tell myself.

I scatter the first three-dollar bag of mulch. A bit of quick math tells me the other nine bags are not going to be nearly enough to make the recommended six-inch-thick layer. I tell myself two inches will have to do.

In the first heavy rain that follows, all the mulch washes down to the bottom of the row and out onto the lawn, through the culvert under the driveway, and across the other lawn, and through a larger culvert and probably all the way to the Mississippi, which I immediately berate myself for polluting. Yes, my decision to get rid of the grass strips was a watershed. Literally.

I think, at this point, about running over the whole garden with the John Deere. Or maybe I should just run over myself with the John Deere. I'm a failure and can't handle all of this, even with the help of several books. I'm also greedy. Just now the daylily row is in full bloom—fifteen different varieties I can count, some of them having several clumps. I don't want to give them up. And I don't know what to do with all of them.

I return to the photographs of English gardens where I notice that the ones which do not have grass paths have beautiful brick paths. The poet Jose Ortega y Gasset once said, "Whoever wants to see a brick must look at its pores, and must keep his eyes close to it. But whoever wants to see a cathedral cannot see it as he sees a brick. This demands a respect for distance."

As I work in the garden, I often consider how passersby view it from the road, a distance of about fifty yards. I perhaps have not distanced myself enough to consider an overall plan, one that will carry the garden through the years to come. I have focused only on the immediate problems. I have reacted instead of being proactive. The idea of building a brick path causes me to take a longer view.

Laying a brick path the length of the garden is not in my budget, but it remains a long-term goal. In the meantime, it makes the cost of a fuzzy landscape fabric that would hold mulch in place better than the slippery black plastic not seem so prohibitive. I bite the bullet and buy two rolls, along with more mulch from the local gas station. I have been such a frequent guest there that the clerks wave when I drive up and don't bother to load the mulch for me.

The new mulch stays in place better, and the new fabric is not as noisy as the plastic was, but it is still unsightly where edges stick out as they seem determined to do no matter where I stake and cover them. Besides this, I have constant anxiety about the next gully-washing rain, and the fact that I am throwing good money after bad by buying more mulch.

The landscape fabric withstands the next rain. Some mulch still washes away but not so much that I go into a total meltdown. Still, I do not like kneeling on wood mulch while I cosmetically weed the irises, which is the only way one can weed them at this point—it just is not possible to get every bit of root out from under those foot-like rhizomes without lifting them, which I am not about to do. I do not like the way crabgrass still manages to find its way to the top of fabric and weld itself in place, its roots gripping the fuzzy fabric in a thousand places. I can put up with all of it, but I do not like it. Maybe grass was better after all?

Having gone this far in my futile attempts to get rid of grasses, I decide that planting more flowers is perhaps the answer. I consider just doing away with the whole path idea and planting some easy-care perennials in between the four problem rows, but even *I* know enough about a garden to know that there is no true easy-care plant. All plants need *some* attention. All plants need food and water.

All plants need freshening and winter care. And there is something about a path, a place to walk among the flowers, which is paradoxically almost the best part of the garden.

A garden is, by definition, plants, but a garden is most fully experienced when one walks through it on a path. Like life, a garden can be enjoyed from the perimeter, but it can only be *known* by getting into it with both feet. I need to be where the daisies tickle my shins and the pink plumes of Queen of the Prairie pat me on the back, because just seeing the garden from the perimeter is like standing in the lobby while a concert is going on in the auditorium. Yes, I might be at the concert, but by walking down the aisle and taking a front-row seat I could see into the singer's eyes, my eardrums would vibrate with the sound, and my nose would sense the subtle scents of the theater itself. In the midst of the crowd, I would make a connection with the place, the performer and the other people. I would receive the gift of being there in that moment.

Walking through a garden is just such a gift. Crawling through a garden for a closer look is such a gift. A garden needs paths, for easy maintenance, to keep weeds at bay, and most of all to offer an invitation. So, if I take away the paths and plant more flowers instead, I will be adding color and variety at the cost of convenience and hospitality. Bad idea. Besides, I've noticed that Brule uses the path instead of tearing down plants as she runs, and I'd like to keep it that way.

I keep the brick walkway idea alive in my mind, but I face the fact that for now I will need to be satisfied with the wood mulch. I have my limits, both in time and dollars. I will have to wear my kneepads, and I will have to keep a kneeling pad in the garden for times when I forget to wear my kneepads. All fine. The wood mulch gives a natural look even if the landscape fabric, which insists on showing itself in too many places, is ugly. I thank it for keeping the weeds somewhat under control and tell myself that I will someday conquer landscape fabric in the same way I conquer quack.

As I am working in the garden one day, a car comes slowly up the drive. I get up to go see who it is. Someone lost, perhaps. Or someone just looking at the garden—people do that sometimes—telling me that other people are seeing my little blooming cathedral from a distance. A man and a woman get out and introduce themselves. They are the people who built our house twenty years ago, who had the 5,000 rose bushes and planted the irises.

I apologize to them for not knowing how to care for roses as they must have, but they are gracious. They even say I seem to be doing a good job. Next they pay me the ultimate compliment of asking if they might take a cutting from an old rose that belonged to one of their grandmothers—one of the few they had been unable to move.

As we walk among the roses, I apologize for the pervading quack. I explain that I don't seem to be a good enough gardener to conquer it. I see the man's eyes light up. He speaks in a hush, like James Bond on a mission: "Have you ever heard of Round-Up? Just apply it around the base of each bush," he says. His wife, standing behind him and out of his sight is shaking her head, "No!"

I listen to the man. I see the woman. And so what should I do? Chemical temptation rears its head in a way that it has not previously, though others have also mentioned chemicals. This man, by virtue of his vast experience and success with roses, holds out a prospect I have been holding out against. He makes it seem so reasonable. So easy. I look at the quack around the roses. The quack in the irises. The quack everywhere. I'm going to have to make another choice: to chemical or not to chemical. I do not have to make it today.

My visitors aren't appalled at the quack, they are entranced by the legacy of the yellow iris row and the lovely peonies, all transplanted from the garden of this woman's mother. Ditto the Siberian irises. The daylilies, they tell me, have been planted by their successor, my friend the master gardener who left all of this behind seemingly just for me. Was she trying to test me? If she was, I suspect she's had a few laughs watching me struggle through the exam.

So it isn't the brick paths that count, or the mulch or even the black plastic, but the trail we leave behind us that makes a difference to others. It is what my predecessors left behind that has led me down paths I never knew I would walk.

Someone once said, "Do not follow where the path may lead. Go instead where there is no path and leave a trail." Such bold thinking. And in the symbolic sense, such a great concept. For the earth, however, I have learned in the washing away of my mulch and the unnaturalness of my landscape fabric that perhaps the kindest thing is to leave no trace at all. To be humble enough to admit that the path we build may endanger all that is displaced by it. In the garden, I want to learn to walk softly, yet I know I leave tracks too, even when I try not to. For this I apologize, and make a mental note to try to do better.

All of my wondering about the previous gardeners on this site, which I thought would be done if I ever got to meet them, has only intensified as I watch them drive away. One says chemicals, one says no chemicals. No one, I realize, can make decisions for me, or answer all of my questions. I'm going to have to find my own way down this path.

Did you ever wonder if you need to consider erosion control in your garden? Unless your garden areas are completely flat, you probably experience some runoff during a heavy rain. It may seem infinitesimal to you, but when added to everybody else's little bit, it becomes a major environmental problem. Water will always seek the lowest level and the easiest way out, so look for tiny channels marking rivulets after a rain—or better yet, go out in the rain (under an umbrella, of course) and see if you can see where water (carrying fertilizer, herbicides, etc.) is escaping. Sometimes a tiny berm is enough to stop the runoff. Sometimes another type of barrier is called for. This is a not a problem—it's an opportunity for you to get creative with borders, paths and groundcovers. You can have fun and save the planet at the same time. Too cool.

# 15

# Too Precious to Plant

R ound-Up. Ever since the day my rosarian friend mentioned the word, I have had it bouncing around in my mind as if it were some new electronic game. This one gives me a little electric shock every time I even think the word. Research reported on the University of Minnesota horticulture website makes me think that I can use this chemical safely. A fertilizer salesman tells me that it's the least harmful of all the "big" chemicals because it doesn't bond with the soil and pollute in the way the others do. All good. Another source says that glyphosate (the chemical in Round-Up) only works for a while, and only under certain conditions.

The university, however, is clear on one thing: never use a rototiller where quack grass is growing. Oh, dear. I have already crossed that bridge, albeit in deep denial. In one of its *Yard and Garden Briefs*, the university goes on to say that "the main thing is to repeatedly eliminate the blades [of quack] by slicing them off with a hoe." This puzzles me. It seems that a rototiller slices things up just the way a hoe does, that tilling is just an easier way of hoeing. Isn't it?

Well, not actually. Tilling uses a circular motion that brings segments of quack root up to the top where they can begin to grow again, as I have already seen. Hoeing cuts the roots off below the soil line. Hoeing repeatedly will eventually starve out the quack roots. Really? I'm skeptical. After all, quack can force itself up through almost anything but concrete. Still, I make a mental note to sharpen my hoe.

The Round-Up game in my head subsides as we begin what the weatherman promises to be a two-week string of ninety-plus-degree days. I'm forced to concentrate on watering. My rose books tell me not to splash water on the leaves (it encourages powdery mildew). Books on perennials tell me to water from the bottom. So much for the gauzy images of gardeners with two-gallon galvanized sprinkling cans. I now approach watering with the same anxiety I have over rototilling. Who knew it was possible to do so many things wrong? How did I ever grow a vegetable garden for so many years without knowing any of this?

Much in the garden wishes to be quietly left alone during this heat, even the trumpet-faced daylilies look as though they won't stand for much more. Every day as I water (before I learn that a deep watering once a week is preferable—along with ten thousand other rules) I watch the small zone four hibiscus I planted in early June for signs that it may cash in its chips early. I think of hibiscus, in general,

as being so delicate they cannot withstand this kind of heat, but this one is not even drooping. At last, a note of encouragement.

Prior to this summer, I have known hibiscus only as houseplants. They have been rare delights, but sometimes difficult houseguests. They have displayed tree-like tendencies soon after arrival, developing woody stems and branching happily upward and outward. They have needed huge amounts of water, so that even if I only watered my other plants once a week I had to make an exception in the case of the hibiscus or its large, showy leaves would wilt so desperately I'd wish I had never brought it home.

Nevertheless, knowing hibiscus to be touchy, touchy, touchy, I had fallen quite deeply in love with a new variety I encountered at the local garden center in June. In a six-inch pot, the plant had one bloom, a magnificent hot-pink, which was larger than my outspread hand. I knew the moment I saw it that even if the hibiscus only ever produced one more bloom it would be worth the $11.99 I had slapped down for it as I ran from the greenhouse before anyone else could get it away from me.

Immediately it became one of those plants too precious to plant. It had to be planted in the perfect place, and suddenly no place looked quite good enough. I searched for several days. The hibiscus sat by the garage, waiting. I feared I might kill it when I planted it, as if there was some strange ritual needed, but I didn't know what it was. I had not yet read Judith Handelsman's book, *Growing Myself,* and learned that asking the hibiscus where it would like to be planted might lead me to an answer.

No, planting this hibiscus was all about me. The rare treasure had to be where everyone would see it—I did want to share that much of it. It had to be where it would not compete with other beauties like the new delphinium. It had to be where it would have the best chance of survival. *Where?*

I carried the pot down to the garden and set it next to the pink phlox. I moved it over by the spiky-quacky irises. I moved it again closer to the roses. Would it be better between two clumps of Russian sage? Beside the pole beans? Where? The hibiscus sat primly alongside the garden for several days while I continued my search for the perfect place, like Da Vinci in search of the perfect model.

One morning, when I saw a bit of yellowing on a leaf, the decision was made in thirty seconds. Plant it anywhere! Just get it in the ground before it dies! And pinch off those precious buds, because they will take energy away from the rest of the plant! I almost wept, knowing that it would not bloom that summer.

Wendell Berry, in his book, *The Unsettling of America: Culture and Agriculture,* suggests that our whole country was brought under cultivation in pretty much this same scenario: people moved in, quickly exploited the land for their own purposes, then moved on. He calls them "the exploiters." Those who do not move on, who stay and pick up the pieces of errant cultivation, over-fertilization, and introduction of unsuitable plant forms he calls "the nurturers." After I so haphazardly planted the hibiscus, I wondered what I was doing. In some kind of gardening dementia that led me to believe the hibiscus was too precious to plant, I certainly had not nurtured it.

Such are the ways we so often proceed, our search for perfection scuttled in the burst of reality that life is not a static thing that sits and waits for us. The hibiscus went into the ground next to some pink phlox and annual asters that, back in June, were still only plants of promise I hoped would not compete too exuberantly with the hibiscus.

For a couple of weeks the hibiscus sat in its new home, still prim, sizing up its neighbors, the buffet, and the ambiance. Then it took off: within a month it was two feet high and climbing—a mountain of green. The ninety-degree weather only seems to encourage this hardy hibiscus, and today as I am bending close to put the hose by its stem, new buds show themselves. I spray my feet.

Once they appear, the buds swell rapidly and then the first flower appears, just as huge and just as pink and, in my mind, even more beautiful than the one the plant had on it at the greenhouse. It is followed by countless others, so many that every day I go to the garden dividing $11.99 by the number of blooms and the plant gets cheaper and cheaper. What a savvy buyer I am! Now I really don't care if the plant makes it through the winter or not. It has cost me no more than a dozen roses at a discount florist and it is lasting all summer. Yet I hope, oh, how I hope, it will be a true perennial.

Every single person who comes, from the UPS man to dinner guests, is dragged down to the garden to see this wonder. I photograph it. I have my husband photograph it. If ever pride could go before a fall, I am sure this is it, but I can't help myself. This plant has been exploited by greed, and is now being nurtured, or exploited, by someone with absolutely no clue as to the proper planting place or procedure, and it has still bloomed. Who could not be proud?

I am so proud that I don't even realize that the reason the hibiscus is blooming so profusely is that it is a tropical plant and it has been waiting all summer for just the kind of hot, steamy weather we are having right now. It has been adapted to withstand zone four winters, but what it really craves is the tropical heat zone four offers in summer—or, as we like to say to Arizonans who come for a visit in July or August, "It's the heat *and* it's the humidity."

Why do I need to try growing this or any other tropical plant? Is it selfishness? Or openness? Some of each, probably. We are asked and allowed to let our reach extend out into the world through gardening. If my plant lives, I will learn that my faith in the rating of the plant as a zone four perennial was justified. If it dies, will I learn that the rating system is false? I think not, though some ratings seem a little too optimistic. Do plants like the hibiscus disturb the natural order of this place I call home, or add to it? New plants offer new opportunities. Sometimes new disappointments too. Not everything is rosy or hot-pink in the garden, or in life.

This specimen, however, radiates hot-pink and now I have a new dilemma: Is it too precious for me to pick a bloom from it? I wonder if all gardeners experience this terrible tension between growing flowers for show and growing flowers for picking. I realize, suddenly, the meaning of the term "cutting garden," but I doubt I would be any more willing to cut there than in any other garden.

A plant in its natural state is almost too beautiful to be disturbed, but I finally convince myself to pick one bloom to find out how long it will last in water, a very minor botanical experiment. The petals touch the edges of a cut glass bowl intended for vegetables or possibly a lovely English trifle. One flower from one plant not yet encased in quack. Untouched by chemicals. I make a mental note to hoe around it with my newly-sharpened hoe, the one in the triangular style my mother always called a "weed hook." I decide to call mine a "quack hook." I feel my back begin to ache. I think of Round-Up.

Did you ever wonder if the Rose of Sharon is the same as the hardy hibiscus? The answer is, well, yes and no. Both are in the hibiscus family, but the Rose of Sharon is a woody shrub, *Hibiscus syriacus* (from Syria?), while the hardy hibiscuses we now buy at the garden center are *Hibisbus moscheutos*. Both plants are hardy to zone 4, and Rose of Sharon is marginally hardy to zone 3. Don't confuse them with *Hibiscus rosa-sinensis*, the gorgeous potted plants you might find at the local greenhouse, but which you might also see in a florist's display. This is the tropical cousin of the first two. Unless you live in zone 7, you'll need to grow it as an indoor plant from first frost to last. Nevertheless, it is a beautiful summertime addition to your potted patio plants. All of the varieties, to my mind, are truly precious.

# 16

# Two Dollars and Forty-nine Cents Well Spent

S ummer is waning as I carry an old lawn chair to the garden one morning, open it up near the roses, sit down, and take in the garden as a whole. I breathe slowly. When working in the garden, I am usually looking down at the ground. If I look to the sky, it may only be to see how much time I might have to run to the house before the storm clouds move in. Today I look at the sky, and I listen.

The living world is playing beautiful symphonies I have been dismissing as elevator music for a long time. Now I hear the motif running through the sounds of wrens, robins, and woodpeckers. My buddy, Brule, rustles through the daylilies. The neighbors' beef cattle moo to each other. A motorcycle with its radio blasting whirs someone off to work.

None of it is startling, or particularly new, but when taken intentionally it is no longer just random noise; it all works to create a pleasing whole that tells me something about this place I call home. As I go off to begin the day's garden tasks and get deep into my own thoughts, it is as though someone has turned off a radio. How adept we are at shutting out the rest of the world.

Poppies grow in my garden, but the opiate I begin to crave is this quiet morning observation time. To work it into my schedule, I make a mental note that tomorrow I will combine it with the time I have usually spent having a cup of coffee at the kitchen table before going outside.

In the following mornings, I see things I haven't before, because now I take time to look for and listen to details. I note the ridges worn around the neighbors' pasture where the beef cattle make their way from where they like to lie under the cottonwoods by the creek to the feed bunks on the other side of the hill. Dead trees. Bent trees. Shrubs that spot the hillsides. Why so spotty? Why here and not there? The way swallows swoop and robins glide. The way sunflowers begin to turn their heads as the sun rises.

Things I have seen before I now see from a different perspective: it is good to take a closer look not just on my knees but face to face with the world, too. I wish that everyone in the world could have the time, or take the time, to do as I am able to do in these few early morning moments. I do not wish on anyone the quack I continue to see looming above the tall perennials.

As I sit in the old aluminum chair one morning, I begin to think of the chair attaining a place of greater permanence, especially if it can be joined by a small table of some kind, a place to set my empty coffee cup and, perhaps, a book. I recall the chimney flues I saw in the woods near one of the compost piles—with a stone or some found object on top, one of them would make the base for a perfect garden table.

The flues are considerably heavier than I expected, but later that morning I haul one down in the wheel barrow and set it beside my chair. Each flue is thirty inches high and twelve inches square. I remember a rectangular piece of salvaged marble from an old dresser that has been waiting in the shed to serve some worthy purpose. It, too, is heavy, but I install it on the top, satisfied that it adds a shabby chic look to the garden, and besides, it will not blow away. The height is perfect. I allow myself a second coffee break to celebrate my success.

Seven more flues wait in a pile in the woods. Their bisque color makes them a natural as bases for clay pots. I haul down two more and install pots of petunias at the edge of what was the vegetable garden before rabbits ate everything, adding both much-needed color and filler, and always-needed vertical lines to the garden. Why didn't I think of this earlier? Even rabbits can't reach the top of these things.

Five to go. One of them, I realize, will become what I have been searching for all summer: the stand for a sundial, a sundial I have seen someone make out of concrete on a gardening show. I have a forty-pound bag of concrete mix in the shed and have been waiting for enough time to work on the project. A sky scan promises another hot afternoon but no rain. Since the garden is too dry for weeding, I decide that even a war on quack has its limits: I can create in concrete with a clear conscience.

Just like on TV, I first assemble the materials: garbage can lid, can of cooking oil spray, wash tub for mixing cement, garden hose, sturdy stir stick and brass rods. I add the cast iron plate from an antique *krumkake* iron (used for making paper-thin, buttery Norwegian delicacies) for good measure. I have been saving it for something, and suddenly this appears to be it.

I mix the concrete, trowel it into the garbage can lid and let it set for a few minutes, then trowel it and lay the *krumkake* iron with its Scandinavian scrollwork design into the center. I set two ten-inch, brass rods tangent to the iron on either side so that they form a ninety-degree angle at the corner, and then I set in a third brass rod at an angle so that it will cast a shadow down onto what is no longer a *krumkake* iron but now the "dial" in "sundial." The concrete cures for twenty-four hours.

To release my creation the next day, I am forced to turn it upside down as if I were removing a layer cake from its pan. Except a cake weighs a few ounces and this weighs forty pounds. Needless to say, I drop the sundial on its face and manage to bend the timekeeping shaft. The TV gardeners didn't tell me about this possible wrinkle, but mostly the fault is mine. Still, the sundial delights me.

Crude and not all that well made, it is my first piece of concrete work. The process encourages me to make more things for the garden. I envision stepping stones, even sculptures. Concrete is cheap, reasonably malleable when wet, and permanent. It is, however, heavy. I make a mental note to learn better ways of removing things from their molds.

My sundial seems to weigh ten times as much as the bag of concrete mix had, but I am eager get it to the garden. Instead of waiting for someone to come home and help me, I drag the sundial the fifty yards alone, then heft it onto one of the chimney flues feeling like Wonder Woman. Who needs to work out at the gym when she can lift weights at home?

After I make sure the flue is straight with the world, I stand back and admire my creation. Not bad. Not great. It will, at least, make a fine alternate place to set my coffee cup. It will also be a good place to put trowels or hand tools when not in use so that they aren't lost under the flowers, which I have already learned can happen. (Where is my dandelion digger?) Even with its bent shaft, my first garden creation will still be put to good use.

A few mornings later, I see the shaft casting a shadow and I am amazed to discover that my sundial might actually tell time, too, if I position it correctly. I set about experimenting to see how this can be done. Research tells me that sundials need to be adjusted for each degree of longitude, and since I have no way to coordinate that, I realize that trial and error will be the best method after all.

I check my watch and turn the concrete disk until the shadow on the dial mimics my watch face. In the adjustment of the dial to align with the sun's movement, I see the importance in and usefulness of observing plant and animal actions more carefully than has been my habit. I see how taking the time to correct something until it works is an actual possibility, not just chance. Wow. All of this from cement and half of a *krumkake* iron.

As soon as the sun is behind a cloud, I realize the fragile nature of this concrete clock. If it is cloudy, there is no timekeeping. If it is a sunny day, the clock will work, but it would work better if I had used a slab of metal rather than a rod for my upright arm, because my quarter-inch diameter rod casts only a very faint shadow. The truth is that since I always wear a watch, I will probably never refer to the sundial anyway. It is an ornament. Something for show. The kind of thing that classy old English gardens have.

Graham Stuart Thomas, my rose expert, cautions me against getting too much of this kind of thing in my garden:

> Our gardens are frequently like a junk shop where a bit of Old Chelsea lies cheek by jowl with a Japanese fan, an elephant's tusk, a piece of modern pottery, or a Roman coin. We are far too prone to go round the garden looking for a site for a new acquisition than to sit quietly and think out the best plant to give effect in a certain place. In the first instance the gardener is a *collector* and the second he is a *selector*, and may well be an artist. Occasionally these two qualities are found in an individual.

Ouch. I already know myself to be a collector, but so far I've contained that vice to inside the house. Am I now going to clutter up the garden too? I don't really need this crude sundial, and I certainly don't need it to work, yet I seem to need it to be there. Its gray surface provides a nice color contrast. Its curves and angles offer different shapes from the lines of the flowers. Its chimney flue pedestal inserts a medium height level between low-growing perennials and tall volunteers like the sunflowers.

The sundial, then, does add a new dimension to the garden, but that is not why I need it there. In its feeble shadow, I already sense that sundials are placed in gardens because they connect us with ancient peoples making discoveries about the world and with their excitement when they realized how something worked, an excitement each of us shares in even the most minor successes in our gardens (not to mention the fact that there is no garden without the sun). In this flawed creation of mine, I share with the ancients, linked across the centuries by the skies above.

Emily Dickinson said, "I dwell in Possibility / A fairer House than Prose." I suddenly know what she meant. The poem ends by saying, "The spreading wide my narrow Hands / To gather Paradise." Unlike Dickinson, I have never linked my soil-caked hands and paradise in the same sentence but now I survey my two dollars forty-nine cents worth of concrete, the found objects my hands stuck into it, and the flowers descended through millions of years of plant genetics. I see the shadow. And I touch the sky.

Did you ever wonder why the sundial is such a common element of garden decor? Gardens tend to be sunny places, and so early time tellers might have placed their sundials there because that was the site of the longest period of sun on their property, hence the place where the clock operated for the maximum amount of time. Now that we no longer tell time by them, we still like the way sundials look in the garden and so there they stay. (Besides, they are no good in the house at all.) Most say we have the Egyptians to thank for this wonderful instrument. Sundials can be accurate to the minute, and up until the nineteenth century they were actually used to check the time on mechanical clocks. (These sundials obviously were not made from krumkake irons . . .) They are considered to be the first scientific instrument, because they added the fourth dimension, time, to what had been, up to then, only a three dimensional world.

# 17

# All Creatures Wanted and Unwanted

**W**hen the young man from the Woodland Stewardship Program appeared at our door, his first question was: "What are your goals for this property?" Did we want to log it off? Certainly not! Did we want to plant Christmas trees? Are you kidding? Did we want to make trails for recreation? Maybe—we like cross-country skiing. Did we want to make habitat for wildlife? Yes—we love wildlife sightings.

Like so many good intentions, ours to create habitat have fallen by the wayside in our pursuit of taming the yard and gardens. We have, however, created a sizeable brush pile from all of the suggested tree trimming. This, at least, will provide a home for something—probably rabbits that will ravage my gardens. My husband reminds me that in winter foxes and coyotes eat rabbits to survive, and they, too, have their place in our little woodland. I'm not so sure, but the brush pile is already in place and can't be burned because conditions are too dry.

I offer a silent invitation to every fox within fifty miles to come visit us. I am afraid of coyotes and invite them to go somewhere else. Likewise skunks and other odious creatures. Mice are invited to remain discreet. I check the ground every time I unload brush and happily see no creatures rushing in and out. We make plans to plant fifty spruce seedlings in an open area in the woods when spring comes. I affirm this as a habitat feature far superior to the brush pile, which I secretly plan to ignite once it is surrounded by snow.

The matter of trails for recreation we talked about with the young man is also forgotten until one Saturday morning in late August when I hear the sound of the chainsaw and see my husband clearing saplings out of a three-foot wide path in the woods just south of the house, the same general area where I made my snowshoe debut in the woods back in February. A second pass through the area with the weed whacker cuts away ferns and gooseberry bushes. After clearing about a hundred yards, my husband walks back down the path, slapping at mosquitoes, ready to quit. He stops in the driveway, turns and looks back at his handiwork.

The newly cleared path looks neat and yet natural. It curves around a huge oak bulging with a burl, it goes under a basswood bent into a rainbow arc by one of the same summer storms that washed all the mulch out from between the problem rows. When I go out for a look, I sense that the new path changes things. There is an opening in what was before almost solid underbrush. No doubt some wildflowers have been cut back before setting seed or whatever it is they need to do to bloom again next spring. Perhaps some oak seedlings have given up their lives.

On the other hand, we now have a way to walk among the trees we need to check on, a path for snowshoeing, and maybe even have a better chance of seeing deer meandering through the woods. It is easy to say that woodlands should be left untouched, but if by not touching them we cannot get into them and get to know them, we will never learn anything about how to take care of them. With this path, we find the woods opened up to us. We will be able to monitor growth patterns, to get on a first name basis with buckthorn, which our Woodland Stewardship book warns us is an invasive species, a weed tree.

As we walk up and down this new path, I wonder how we will ever get rid of all of the box elders and elms on the property if they are weed trees, too. Every other tree I look at seems to be a box elder or an elm. I do not even know how to identify buckthorn yet, but no doubt there are many of them too. Like quack, these weed trees cannot be killed by cutting—they re-sprout from the roots. Where one tree stood formerly with a single trunk, the new tree will have dozens of new trunks. If I do not do better with trees than I have been doing with quack, our woods will be overtaken by weed trees in no time.

Summer heat and mosquitoes save me from pondering this horror at length. The path is beautiful, but will be more useful after the first frost has killed off some of the bugs. For the time being, it offers an invitation I decline. The woods will have to take care of themselves. I will take care of the yard and garden. That is the bargain I make. Separate but mostly equal. I realize that the Woodland Stewardship people envision and accept human interference in woodlands, and in some cases even welcome it.

In fact, the first page of the stewardship plan booklet quotes Aldo Leopold's *A Sand County Almanac,* stating, "conservation is a state of harmony between men and land." (Not women, but, okay, I get the point.) Balance. I like that. We can never, possibly, cut all of the box elders, elms, or buckthorn. We must do what we can, create habitat where we can, and trust nature to know considerably more than we do. Harmony is the goal. Yet it is not harmony I feel.

The first walk on this new path, though peaceful, has produced new sources of anxiety that send me back to the Woodland Stewardship book in search of answers. In a section called "Forest Facts," I learn that each American uses the equivalent of a 100-foot tree each year in the form of newspapers, tissues, paper towels, furniture, building materials, and such. Each of these trees takes about sixty years to grow. Each mature tree has approximately 120 pounds of leaves and produces about 5,000 seeds that will launch themselves on the wind and plant themselves in suitable spots.

The image of the box elder clump I saw growing serenely beside the path morphs into a box elder jungle I can't even walk through. I have the knee-jerk reaction that we should just clear the whole woodlot and plant Christmas trees, the way the young man suggested, but it passes as quickly as it comes. We will cope, somehow, with box elders. I do not say how.

The Stewardship booklet includes fact sheets on buckthorn, exotic honeysuckles, black locust and Siberian elms—all harmful, invasive species. I take a closer look at the pictures of Siberian elm and am aghast to realize that I have two of them growing at the top end of my perennial/rose garden, forming what I have, up to now, thought was a lovely backdrop and a quiet spot for my aluminum lawn chair. Wrong again.

According to the experts, the trees should go. Maybe they are even worse than quack? Is anything worse than quack? Something in me doubts it. I read that Siberian elms provide significant habitat for birds, so they are fulfilling part of our

Stewardship plan. We start with baby steps. And denial. Because maybe the Siberian elms much prefer birds to humans.

What are our goals for the property? This I ask as I consider the new path and what it has opened to us. We have seen deer, but Brule sees to it that they don't come too near the flowers, a feat of spaniel strength I thank her for each time I hear another gardener tell of a deer rampage through the hostas. So far my hostas are just fine, despite the occasional slug. But goals, real goals? The very thought of that fans fears I haven't faced because I don't want to make the wrong decision. Setting goals forces us to look years down the road, not just to the next blade of quack grass needing to be hoed. Planning for trees requires commitment.

It is far easier to plant perennials, some of which have only a three- or four-year lifespan, than actually to commit to a long-range plan for one's life and one's place. Fear grips me anew as I consider this. What if I continue to do so many things wrong? What if I make the wrong choices, plant the wrong trees, maybe even kill off the last remaining endangered species in our woods because I am too ignorant to know what it is? Responsibility sits heavily on my shoulders. What will create harmony for all in this habitat? Perhaps not the fire I'm planning.

The new path has opened up more than just the woods. It has made me see that managing this new place for the next generation is going to take some planning. I wonder if there is room for me, too, to take refuge under the brush pile.

Did you ever wonder how to burn a brush pile safely? First, check for burning restrictions in your city or township. You may not be able to burn at all. Sorry. If burning is allowed, it may only be allowed at certain times of the year. If your brush pile is huge and you worry it might burn out of control, you may need to contact your local fire department for assistance. Of course the other way, which requires more work on your part, is to pull pieces off from the big pile to burn in a small, controllable, area. Watch for fleeing creatures as you work. I like to wear tall boots for this activity.

# 18

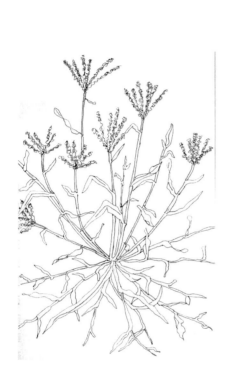

# In the Time of Tiger Lilies

I was probably no more than four or five when I first asked what those orange flowers in the road ditches were, and someone told me that they were tiger lilies. The image of a terrifying tiger in one of my picture books leaped before my eyes, and I immediately feared the flowers were going to turn into ferocious beasts. Needless to say, I never forgot the name. I now wish I could find such an easy mnemonic for every flower, especially for the Latin names with which I am slowly beginning to acquaint myself. *Filipendula. Baptisia. Lavandula.*

I started to watch for the gawky bright orange flowers during long car trips while my father wheeled along in a string of 1950s Oldsmobiles, smoking Camel cigarettes and looking everywhere but at the road. If friends were along on the ride, often someone else's father was smoking a cigar. I stayed in the back seat, the early non-smoking section, and tried desperately to fight off car-sickness (never successfully) by looking only at the road ahead instead of out the side window (also never successfully—motion, after all, is motion).

Few flowers can be identified at eighty-five miles per hour, my father's preferred cruising speed. Tiger lilies, however, are bold enough to be seen at any speed, if only as a blur. Their color is the epitome of late summer in the Midwest: an orange so hot I wish I could escape it, an orange that reminds me of the gorgeous colors just ahead when the leaves turn. These lilies do not last long before fading to brown as autumn approaches. They are as common as weeds. Some people probably consider them weeds. To me, by size, color, and habit, and especially by the magic of their name, they are every inch a flower. *Lilium.*

I ride the lawn mower on a late August day when the lawn is burning up and only the crab grass, quack grass and dandelions are green. The John Deere must look like a big green bug to the red-tailed hawk that soars overhead. He circles back for a better look. We see each other but go our own ways, each having a job to do. I try not to visualize the major part of his, which is obtaining food—and I don't mean seeds and berries.

As I roll along in the middle of the lawn where there is no trimming to contend with, I scan our road ditch for tiger lilies. They do not disappoint. There they are, dotting the dull, tan, and khaki grasses with blazing brightness.

An ocean away, England is home to tiger lilies, too. The ones I remember most vividly grew at a bed-and-breakfast in Wales where we found ourselves one evening at the end of a long day's drive to Hay-on-Wye. No reservations. We just happened onto it. We found room at the inn—a four-hundred-year-old fieldstone farmhouse with walls a foot thick. It was run by a woman named Emma who told us she had always wanted to travel the world, but her husband wanted only to stay home and tend his cows along with the occasional thoroughbred horse he could afford to buy. Since she couldn't leave, she decided to open the B&B and let the world come to her.

At the time we visited, the B&B had been open for eleven years. The husband had been dead for the last five of those. Emma had had guests from over eighty countries and had made peace with the fact that she was never going to travel out of the United Kingdom. She had five sleek thoroughbreds grazing in her paddock. There, among her tiger lilies, she was not just content, but totally at peace—and so we were, too. Did she close her eyes as she told me her story, I wonder, or is it just that I remember it that way?

Lawn mowing is a great thinking activity, I decide, as my John Deere bobs along and the tiger lilies make orange exclamation points across the road. I remember the ones in Wales and think how nice it would be to feel at peace the way Emma seemed to. One wheel of my tractor lines up with the last cut and I make another circle. I am circling like the hawk, and my mind is hungry for answers just like the hawk is hungry for—his next victim.

What might my next victim be? As I look over the green tufts of quack grass springing up in the mulched areas and the quack still permeating the irises, I know only too well what it should be.

The newly cut lawn is golf course smooth if not fairway watered. It sets off the long problem rows, the teardrop-shaped vegetable/flower garden, and the roses beautifully except that the quack in the irises continues to be more than just unsightly. It is peace-destroying. I realize as I circle around and around that I should try an experiment: dig up the showy, bearded iris rhizomes in the V-shaped flower bed where there are *only* two twenty-foot rows, de-quack it, and then replant it. If this experiment goes well, I can tackle the long rows later. I'll eat the elephant bite by bite, as they say.

The concept is so simple that I don't know why I didn't consider it earlier. Well, maybe I know: the quack in this bed hadn't looked as threatening earlier in

the summer. Now it looks every bit as bad as it does in the long problem rows, but there is not as much square footage that requires digging. I will give it a try and make an informed decision. Having hit on this plan of attack, I feel light enough to ride a thermal spiral right up there with the hawk and soar around for a while. He has given up on me, though, it seems, and the sky is empty.

Why didn't I just decide this earlier, I ask myself once I realize how peaceful I feel with a plan of action before me at last. Maybe I doubted I could wage a war with quack and win? Maybe I was just lazy? Maybe I just wanted to keep my options open? Whatever the reason, the decision seems as full of life as those vivacious tiger lilies. Surely this is how Emma felt when she announced her decision to open the B&B.

I stop the John Deere right in the middle of the lawn when I see the hawk come back and land near the top of a dead box elder tree across the road. Will he make a sound? Might I hear his wings as he preens, or flies? Everything is quiet now that the noisy engine has stopped. I hear the cardinal call to his mate. I hear crickets—probably chewing on something in the garden. I hear the bellow of a neighbor's cow, but I can't tell which neighbor. It doesn't make any difference: it's a lovely sound. The hawk remains silent. His decision. I accept it and put my hand on the key to start the tractor again.

Just as I put in the clutch, I look up to see if the hawk is still there. He is. And he's not watching me. He's hunting the road ditch. He's looking for what scampers beneath the tiger lilies, but I suspect he sees the flowers too, and I wonder if he enjoys them as I do. I wonder if he has a history with them, as I do in my childhood memories? As I look at him, I am flooded with the sense that he has a history every bit as important as my own. We share this time of tiger lilies, and so much more.

Later that week, I read up on "lifting" irises, and I begin my task in the small iris bed. I realize I should have lifted the rhizomes years earlier. This bed contains many varieties of large, bearded hybrids I want to save. It also contains many lesser yellows and purples I think I might just throw down in the ditch with the tiger lilies. As I am on my knees in the sun, digging up irises, I come to the full realization that this task is going to take *days*. Just then, a neighbor I have not met before drives in.

I have heard from other neighbors that she is a gardener *extraordinaire*, and I shudder at what she's going to say about my quack mess, but she is gentle. She notes that she does not have any quack in her gardens but that her sister, who does, uses a paintbrush dipped in—here it is again—Round-Up, to selectively eradicate it. I look at the amount of quack in just this one garden and calculate how long (and how much Round-Up) it would take. I smile and allow that I might try.

When the irises finished blooming back in June, I had managed to tie pieces of orange string around the stalks of the varieties I wanted to save. Now that it is August, most of the strings are either gone or so far down into the quack that I can't see them. Some are uncovered as the lifting begins, but I know as I sort the rhizomes into "save" and "discard" piles, I'm getting rid of some that I should save. The big blue-and-white variety has rhizomes identical to the puny purple variety.

So much of gardening is about what can't be seen, which is why I think it has such endless appeal. Sometimes the gardener is a magician, but more often he is more like the woman in the box being sawed in two—just a prop.

The discard pile grows larger and larger. I grow uneasier and uneasier over how to dispose of the extras. Maybe I can find a place for some of these in another garden, I think. Then I remember that I don't want any more irises. But still…When I finish lifting irises from both rows and cleaning away all signs of quack, I till the badly compacted soil (continuing my denial that tilling is a bad thing) and replant about half of the irises, including some from the discard pile.

After that, I give irises away to anyone who will take them, reminding them to wash the rhizomes well before planting because I cannot guarantee I've gotten all of the weeds out of them. My quackless neighbor, who had dropped in the day the experiment began, declines to take any. This tells me a great deal about why she does not have quack in her garden.

Some rhizomes, of course, are left without homes. I am unable to dump them in the ditch, even knowing that they might be able to commune with the tiger lilies, and so I begin to find places for them here and there in the garden, around the bases of tree trunks, at the edge of the woods—anyplace I can work the ground. I will accept whatever comes of it all, I tell myself. I wonder if Mr. Thomas, my rose expert, would classify me as a *collector* or a *selector* until it occurs to me that I am a *propagator.*

Dividing and replanting are ways of propagating a species. They are also an insurance policy against having given away the wrong plants. I smile. I *am* doing something right, even if I now have even more irises to keep weeded.

The newly-dug bed looks so neat and clean that I know it will please the hawk, should he take a circle over the grounds again anytime soon. He will be able to see a field mouse running through it now when he couldn't have in the days of the quack-mire. For now, the bed looks quack-free. Then I look across the road to the tiger lilies and I see what I didn't see at age four: there is no tiger in the tiger lily.

Did you ever wonder why tiger lilies are orange? It turns out the lily growing in the ditches everywhere in the Midwest isn't a tiger lily at all. It is *Lilium superbum* (Turk's Cap Lily). True tiger lilies are recognized for their broad, slightly curved petals dotted with black spots. Roadside lilies usually lack the spots. So now, not only is there no tiger in my tiger lily but there is also no lily in it . . . So anyway, why orange? The simple answer is that they just are. The longer version is that they contain carotene, which is a pigment that absorbs blue and indigo light leaving us with rich yellows and oranges. Carotene is important to the human diet, as the human body breaks down each carotene molecule to produce two vitamin A molecules. Perhaps this is why daylily bulbs are eaten in many parts of the world, especially the Far East. Daylilies—they're not just for bouquets anymore.

# 19

# Raspberry Fields Forever

I knew at the beginning that the raspberry patch was way more than I could handle. With picturesque wooden posts, three fifty-foot rows of brambles taunted me from the south end of the lawn: "Come on out here and try to pick every last berry. We dare you!"

Busy with moving and renovating, I had found it easy to ignore the whole patch in October. Still busy with the house, and then the gardens, I hired the former handyman for the place to come and help cut out the dead canes in the spring. This turned out to be nearly a two-day job for the two of us. When the first crop of berries hung heavy on the canes in July, our teenaged son took over, picking berries in the morning and marketing them in a nearby town in the afternoon, selling out each day. After ten days of sweat, mosquitoes, scratches, and purple fingers he had had enough of raspberries. I managed to pick a few. We ate berries, gave berries away, and still let many go to waste.

Guilt grips me once again now that it is September. Our son is back in school, leaving me no chance of cajoling him into another round with the berries. I anticipate the sickeningly-sweet coconut smell of the unpicked, overripe berries I remember from last October when we were moving in. Here I am, once again awash in what most people hoard as a gourmet delicacy, but unwilling to make use of it. I do not let my eyes veer in the direction of the blackberries and elderberries that line the edges of the woods. Even the birds can't eat all of them.

As the rest of the garden begins to shrink in the late summer heat, steeling itself against dormancy, the raspberries, many of them seven feet tall and drooping with berries that have turned from moss-green to off-white to pink and which now promise to swell to the size of ping pong balls, tell me I will have to get out there and get picking if I am any kind of person at all. I succumb to the premise that I am not.

Instead, I use the excuse that I need to wallpaper the library while our daughter is home from college to help and she will only be home this one weekend. We strip off the old wallpaper, not a fun job but much better than picking raspberries. Wallpapering together goes smoothly—she fastidious and tall, I speedy and short. It is while she is smoothing out the top of a long strip and I am supporting the lower section that she mentions that there are lots of ripe raspberries. "They'll just have to wait," I tell her. They can just rot away for all I care, I think.

We hang another sheet of marbleized wallpaper I chose because it looks like the inside cover of an antique book. All I can see is the raspberry color that swirls between a deep-green and deep-blue. I think of the raspberry patch I should be caring for it.

*Next spring*, I tell myself as I slice away the excess paper along the ceiling beams with a single-edged razor blade. I will cut the dead canes and trim every live one back to its top green leaf. I will fertilize with composted cow manure. I will till the soil—only a little—then mulch it to help keep weeds down. I will stake the canes by tightening the long wires between those rustic wooden posts. I will have the most glorious raspberry patch in Minnesota. And I will pick the berries. Every last one of them. I will meet their dare. And raise them, so to speak.

And then I tell myself this probably isn't true, but that I *am* going to eliminate every last raspberry plant that has crept out into the middle of the rows and all of those trying to form new rows along the outside. Well-spaced plants produce more than crowded ones anyway, though more production is not really my desire. In fact, maybe I should just leave the whole thing alone.

Later in the week, after our daughter returns to school, the berries are still hanging there, a warm streak having ripened them all at once. I pick some along the outside edges of the patch where I won't get scratched. Eating as I pick, I decide the autumn berry crop is, if anything, better than the July crop. And there are fewer berry bugs. I try to be thankful. As the extreme boredom of endless picking sets in, I realize what a great job our son did in slogging through so many quarts during the July crop.

Surrounded by lethal raspberry thorns, I imagine how nice it would be to have a berry patch of manageable size, maybe five feet by five feet, just enough to provide a bowl of perfectly ripe fruit. Perhaps I should just mow down the canes and admit I can't cope with this. Perhaps I should mow down all but one row. Or one cane.

I consider these options, then remember the raspberry patch we had where we lived before. It had started out as two nice rows of berries and had gradually turned into a weedy mess I couldn't stand. When I tried to reduce it to a manageable size, I ended up killing the whole thing. Conscience does not allow me to contemplate a repeat of that performance and I decide to let this patch live out its life unharmed. To cope the best I can. To enlist the help of my family whenever I can. To remember that it is not just *my* berry patch, but *our* berry patch. To remember that quack isn't nearly as unsightly here as it is in the irises, and the raspberries certainly can hold their own against it.

The September morning is crisp and bright the next day as I walk into the patch again, canes up to my neck and some over my head, berries juicing against my pale blue shirt as I work my way down the rows. I wear an old belt perfect for just this purpose, and onto it is strapped an ice cream pail, which I fill before I get halfway down the row. I can fill several more if I wish. I pick the largest, most perfect berries for my breakfast, yet I see that I am one against many. I am a toy boat bobbing on a sea of raspberries. When I consider the odds of my getting out of the patch without any scratches, I sense how Geraldine Ferraro must have felt when contemplating her chances of becoming the first female vice-president of the United States.

Before the first berries cover the bottom of the second pail, I already hope that some of the people I've invited to come and pick berries will actually take me up on the offer, but I know few, if any, will. People are busy and berry picking takes time. I question my priorities. After all, should raspberries be a priority—for me, or anybody? Should we always make time for what is given to us or should we be discriminating? Do we even have a choice?

After a couple of days of picking, I have beaten down a path, albeit an overgrown path, among these berries. I have made berry picking an unpleasant task because I did not clear the path when I should have. I did not keep down the weeds with mulch as I know I should have. I did not get the wires in place in time to support the tall canes. So I should not blame the raspberries. I should blame myself—I who have thought my other pursuits much more important than caring for raspberries. Am I right? Do I not owe them some of my time?

Because I am a human, am I by definition more valuable than a raspberry cane? I certainly have always thought so, but now I find that the raspberries hold the power. I see that I am just one picker in the field of life. Raspberries are going to make themselves my priority twice each year. I can either ignore them and feel guilty forever, or I can cooperate by back-breaking pruning and weeding which will in some ways make my picking easier. Another decision required. I decide to wait and make it later.

In the meantime, I pick. I'm adept at pulling the tall asters that get in my way (and know I have to get my pail out of the way first or I will have tiny white petals all over my berries). I can ease the tangle by cutting off a single grapevine that is using the canes for a soft trellis. Maybe these raspberries, like the irises, do not need to be an either/or kind of proposition? Maybe there is an easier way? That would be to ignore them. Again.

---

Did you ever wonder why some raspberries are called everbearing? (I didn't say *overbearing*, although I might have thought it.) Maybe it's because it seems like you have to pick them forever? Actually, it is because there are two types of berries, the other being called summer bearing—the kind that fruits only once per year on second year canes. The everbearing varieties fruit both in midsummer and in late summer/early autumn. Also, the everbearing varieties can fruit on the first year canes (lightly) as well as on the second year canes (profusely). Either way, raspberries are delicious—if difficult.

---

# 20

## In Sherwood Forest

Most gardeners rue the coming of winter, at least publicly. After a year as a more-or-less full-time gardener, I now suspect some of that rue to be fabrication. I, for one, am going to sigh with relief when there is nothing more to be done outside—especially picking raspberries. When the ground is frozen and I can't hoe even if I want to. When I can put my feet up on the ottoman and read a good book. I won't think about the garden all winter.

Winter, however, has not yet come. October has blown in with some leaf-piling winds and cold nights, but the ground is far from frozen. I have dahlia and gladiolus bulbs, calla lilies and cannas to dig—tasks I know how to do and can attack with vigor. One question, though, continues to nag me: What am I going to do with the rest of irises?

The small iris bed took the better part of three days to dig, clean and replant. The irises have put up new shoots and seem happy, but a few spears of telltale quack have also bullied their way back. Is it worth lifting the whole, long row of yellow irises only to have the same thing happen there?

Somehow that long row of quacked-in irises has become a litmus test for the garden. If I dig it up and clean it out, I am committing myself to major gardening which goes against the agreement my husband and I made when we moved in. (No fussy gardens! Not us!) If I destroy it, well, I destroy something beautiful. The idea is painful. I hear the adage "no pain, no gain" ring in my ears, but what will I gain from the pain of lifting those hundreds of rhizomes?

I will gain more work and a sore back. I will gain newly sprouted quack. But then, of course, there will be that week in June when I will walk in yellow heaven. *If I suffer the pain of losing this beauty, what will I gain?* Time. Precious time. And a victory over quack because, if I destroy the irises, I will convert that space back into lawn, where quack is not an issue.

The second-floor loft in the house provides a bird's-eye view of a plot of woods that separates the house and the gardens. I stand at the window on a football-weather kind of morning, contemplating whether my tasks for that day should include taking some action on the irises. Unwilling to decide, I focus instead on the yellow poplar leaves that rustle against a clear, blue sky. Tall, white trunks sway gently in the breeze not fifteen feet from the window. Squirrels leap from basswood to cherry to cottonwood. Woodpeckers drill and chip. The forest is alive and ever-changing. Only I seem to be stalled.

Three massive cottonwood trees, their trunks nearly three feet in diameter and their leaves already gone, stand between me and the four problem rows. The cottonwoods' sheer hulk reminds me of the giant oaks we saw on the trip to England when our teenagers were determined to see Sherwood Forest. Not Windsor Castle. Or Big Ben. Or Buckingham Palace. No, Sherwood was what they wanted. I prepared myself for a spendy tourist attraction as I white-knuckled my way up the British freeway, hanging onto the far left lane for dear life.

Sherwood, of course, turned out to be quite super-natural. Its huge expanse of woodland runs smack through a dense population area, and its eight-hundred-year-old trees are so large their limbs have to be supported by man-made frameworks. Every gnarly limb has faces in its bark, faces that growl or smile or smirk. The actual Robin Hood tree is like an apartment house, each limb large enough to support a family of four and it is not a problem to picture Robin Hood, Little John, and the merry men hiding there in complete safety.

Now, seeing the tops of my own cottonwood trees at eye level and thinking about Sherwood, I wonder what it would be like to leap out onto one of the broad, horizontal branches, and I sense again that real, supernatural power I experienced in Sherwood. Maybe it's because I've never really been so up close and personal with a treetop before that I am struck now by what amazing plants trees are. Or maybe it is that today I see the cottonwoods in comparison to the bothersome iris row beyond them.

My worries over foot-high irises seem minor in comparison with these giants. Why haven't I stood in awe of their size, their abilities, and their gifts of shade and habitat each and every day of my life? I make a mental note to pay more attention.

Thinking one can know a tree by just looking at its trunk is like thinking one can know a man by looking only at his shins. These trees are growing to over a hundred feet without so much as the touch of my hand, and are probably the better for it. From my perch in the loft, I have not only a closer look, but I am taking that look from a new perspective. Yes, I am small in relation to these behemoths, but I *am* in relation to them. It seems the irises may have stalled me on purpose just so I could take this closer look. I must remember to thank them, quack and all.

These cottonwood trees are not large by Sherwood Forest standards, where the major oak, a.k.a. the Robin Hood tree, has a circumference of thirty-three feet. Our woodlot was logged several decades back, so the trees are younger, and there is a great deal of underbrush, including the predatory buckthorn, which makes me wonder once again if my fixation on the irises and quack should be my main concern. Shouldn't I be concentrating on the forest, which, properly maintained, might someday be another Sherwood?

In 1962, Minnesota launched a Big Tree Hunt to find the state's largest native trees. A quick scan of the list tells me that none is located in Goodhue County, where I live, but that the largest black walnut tree in the state is located in a backyard just ten miles away in the next county. Tree envy grips me, but more than that, tree respect fills me.

Considering what might be done to help these noble creatures, I take an even closer look. One branch is growing parallel to the ground with a half-dozen waterspouts growing out of it. I know from my rose pruning books that they should fall to the saw. A fallen tree has caught a sapling in its web and calls for release. A dead tree has fallen across another path my husband made for me between the shade garden and the nearest compost bin, and so I want to open up that too. Deadfall needs clean up and brush piles need burning. Perennials need cutting, bulbs need digging, tools need winterizing. What does the iris row need?

The cottonwoods challenge me to rethink the irises. A cottonwood's lifespan will never rival that of an oak, but aren't they and their eight-foot-circumference trunks worthy of my attention? If I don't give it, won't urban sprawl or the need for a few more acres of corn get the better of them and their kind? Won't some busybody like me who wants everything to look like a garden have them taken down in favor of a tree hydrangea or Japanese maple?

Each life is precarious, subject to winds and whims and weather. Each life. Cottonwood. Iris. Even mine. I may not be able to save or tend it all, but I see that the need for care extends beyond the limits of a simple garden.

This day, however, it is what the trees have shed that is called to my attention. Leaves. Great drifts of leaves now cover the lawn (and the quack!), trumping my conflict over the irises. Our garden tractor has a vacuum attachment that saves leaf clean-up from being an impossible task, and as I climb up onto the bright yellow seat, I make a mental note to try to think up a machine that can save digging irises from being an impossible task.

All day, I mow and vacuum, dumping the bags of chopped leaves and grass in my compost bins until they overflow and I have to start a new pile. Then another. Climbing roses are freed from their trellises so that they can begin to lie down for their winter's nap, and mountains of leaves are piled next to them and the other roses so they can all be covered when the time is right.

The next day I dig bulbs. Gladioluses and dahlias are set to dry on newspapers in the garage before their winter storage in the basement. I wind grapevines into wreaths, too, while I'm at it, freeing up a row of lilac bushes that spent the summer bending, like the raspberries, from the weight of the fast-growing vines. I cut some bittersweet. I put away plant supports and shovels that have come to rest at various points around the various gardens. I clean up apples from under the apple trees and walk past the raspberries, thankful that they are finally done for the year, once again promising I will do better next year.

The next day, I empty the bird baths and turn them upside down to keep them from breaking when they freeze, as they now do every night. Already I begin to wish for spring. I drain the hoses, roll them up, put them away. I put away the

martin-house picnic table and the lawn chairs. I empty pots. I haul away plant foliage by the trailer load. I bring in wood for the fireplace.

As autumn activity races toward the freeze-up deadline, I talk to no one but carry on the dialogue I have been having for a whole year. It is October 15 again. We have lived at the new house one whole year. For one whole year I have been asking myself what I should do about the quack in the irises. *One whole year.* I look at the long row of irises, quack growing in and around them as if no one has tended this garden all summer, and I know that today is the day.

Lao-Tsu said, "The journey of a thousand miles begins with a single step." Mine is a step on the shovel. Actually it's a jump on the shovel, with both feet. The ground is not frozen, but it is hard—after all, it is basically sod. My inner kangaroo goes crazy. I jump and kick the shovel down hard, wincing at the sight of every white quack root, especially the ones I cut. I throw whole clumps of quack and irises into the wheelbarrow, my plan being to get it all out of there, till the soil and replant the viable rhizomes. Most clumps need to be pried apart by two garden forks. Some are so heavy I can't lift them. I settle for dragging them off onto the lawn and keep on going.

When my son comes home from school, I enlist his help. While we work, we talk about school, and basketball, and why on earth I would want to dig up this whole long row and why he should have to help. This conversation goes on for several days until the whole row is dug and great heaps of iris rhizomes lay piled beside the garden. I admit, the evil thought that I should just leave them there and let them freeze crosses my mind, but only for a minute.

As I sit on the ground prying, sorting and discarding the last of the irises, I try to answer my son's question about why I am doing this odious task when I know that perhaps even before the first snow flies tiny bits of quack will be asserting themselves on my field of honor. *What has possessed me to do this?* Now I am committed to cleaning up the peonies and daylilies and Siberian irises too. Be careful what you wish for. Well, I wished for this big, beautiful place in the country and I got it. I didn't wish for quite so much work, I think, yet I feel energized by doing it. Cold, but energized. Now I am wishing for a yellow blaze in June.

Not long after I complete the task, I retire to the loft, flop down in front of the TV, and flip through the channels. *Robin Hood* with Errol Flynn is playing on TCM. Hollywood's version of Sherwood Forest is a dark, overgrown place the Sheriff of Nottingham and all of his men can't even find their way into. Outside my window, the cottonwood trees form eerie silhouettes. One of them has two branches that stick out at right angles opposite each other so that the tree looks like a giant about to grab me. In the half darkness, it looks every bit as menacing as those in Errol Flynn's Sherwood Forest. It seems to have a face, just the way the Robin Hood tree did. So do its merry buddies.

While I have been tending gardens, digging irises and cleaning up leaves, I have been totally oblivious to individual tree specimens. Now that the leaves are gone, I see them not as a mass of green shade trees, but as unique species, different in shape, in bark, and in habits. I am surprised to find myself thinking that I like them better as skeletons than as green-leaved summer friends because now I see their core, their heart, their very soul. I am very sorry I have ignored them for most of my life.

Humans have a need to give human attributes to other species in order to relate to them, and so seeing faces on gnarled trees helps us relate to them in ways we don't otherwise. I chide myself for my all-too-human arrogance in thinking that I can/should help the trees, when, in fact, they are the ones helping me in ways I cannot see, like providing oxygen (duh), so, therefore, have not applauded. Yet we exist here together, all of us now stoically preparing for the coming of winter. Ready to settle in and wait for the yellow blaze of bloom from next spring's iris crop, I will put my feet up on the ottoman and read a good book, but I will be watching the tree tops for signs of spring.

So, perhaps gardeners truly do rue the coming of winter. I admit publicly that I may have been wrong about them.

Did you ever wonder if we have any trees like the Robin Hood Tree here in the U.S.? We have the General Sherman Tree. One of the giant California sequoias, it was named after General William Tecumseh Sherman by one of his former lieutenants in 1879. This caused some discussion over which was larger, General Sherman or another sequoia, the General Grant Tree. Currently, Sherman is winning the war. There are four California redwoods so large you can actually drive a car through them (no longer considered environmentally chic, with good cause . . .) The U.S. Forest Service maintains a Big Tree Register, and invites nominations for new trees to add to its list. Its website tells us that trees "sequester carbon dioxide, trap pollutants, and clean the air and water." All that, Robin Hood, and generals, too. Not all the stars are in Hollywood.

# 21

# Dead Things

The new iris row shudders, a few brown eyelashes peeking out from under a thin layer of late November snow. I am pretty sure I've killed all twenty-four circles of twenty rhizomes each I so laboriously planted too late in the season. Almost all of the spiky leaves, which I cut down to the four-inch high fans recommended by my books, are dry and shriveled. I did not heed the calendar, or the weather signs, and now I have killed all of the yellow irises. On every trip to the garden, or walking past it to go to the mailbox, or at any odd moment during the day, I berate myself for mass murder.

A week after Thanksgiving, snow blankets my world as Brule and I walk down the driveway to get the mail. She veers off to run up one of the garden paths, fresh snow flying up with every footfall. Her pretty, spaniel nose burrows down in search of mice or moles. Under the snow I can see the outline of the four long S-shaped rows: irises and all the rest. I can see the outline of the teardrop garden. Stems of perennials not adequately cut down in the autumn stick up through the snow looking like they have been dipped in sugar and I make a mental note to leave more things standing next year.

Details I had not seen on those plants all summer stand out now in the crystalline white. The small arbor vitae shrubs I planted last spring make pleasing mounds of green with tiny icicles. The shrub roses still hang onto some leaves and their many rose hips attract birds the way the bird bath does in summer. Unfortunately, unbothered by the cold, quack is busy building strong bones and muscles, training for next spring's marathon.

My eyes go back, as they always do, to the iris row. I try to imagine what it might look like in the coming spring if I had just left it alone instead of killing it off with my compulsive October digging. The irises were really quite beautiful, despite the quack. It strikes me as I look on the row now that it was not for the irises I went through all of that labor and lifting—it was for me. It was to make *me* look good, not the plants. I wanted people to think I am a better gardener than I actually am. The problem with the irises was a problem because I made it one. Impetuosity and pride in appearances led to the war on quack that resulted in the annihilation of hundreds of rhizomes. It occurs to me that this same dynamic works to make all wars so futile: we attempt to remake someone or someplace else into our image of what they should be when we can never all be the same—and shouldn't be.

My quack battle failed because I neglected to plan for the imminent onset of winter. Or for the lack of rain in late autumn. Or for how compacted the soil becomes after a summer of pounding rains. Or for the nature of the irises themselves, who like to be transplanted a little earlier, thank you. I also neglected to get to know the growing habits of quack. I should have observed how deep the roots went, the directions they took, the kinds of soil they liked. Instead, I made assumptions. Needless to say, most of my assumptions were wrong. I make a mental note to review my list of mental notes.

Despite my guilt over the probable iris deaths, I realize that an intense summer in the garden has helped me approach death with a less fearful heart. Observing the lives and deaths of plants, and especially of this endless row of irises, brings the important reminder that life is short and fragile. Broken robin's eggs in late spring reminded me that squirrels and blue jays have different priorities from mine.

In the still-slimy baby rabbit which Brule brought to me in early summer, I saw evidence that nature carries on despite my many misguided attempts to fix everything—a lesson I should have learned when I was in my twenties and my husband brought home twin Jersey calves only two days old.

The calves had no economic value to the farmer. The female, Kelly, would have been infertile because she had a male twin, and the male, the one we named Gus, looked weak. Their chances for survival were limited at best, but my husband and one of his veterinary partners bought them for ten dollars, thinking we might be able to raise at least one of them and provide our families with a freezer full of beef. I was appointed to take care of them, even though I knew nothing of raising calves. Despite frantic calls to my mother-in-law for advice (What do you do for scours? How much do I feed them? Help!) and plenty of antibiotics, Kelly died within forty-eight hours.

Finding Kelly, her little black body cold and stiff, her tongue looking large and out of place, frightened me so that I went screaming silently from the old brooder house, where the cattle operation was housed, all the way up to the house where I immediately called my husband to come home and do something.

What did I want him to do? Well, of course, I wanted him to bring her back to life. To give her a shot that would make her stand up and drink again. Instead he said gently that there was nothing to be done and that Gus would probably follow shortly. By night, Gus was gone too. It was my mother-in-law, who had so lovingly raised calves, children, and gardens, who made the whole thing bearable for me when she said, "Death is a beautiful thing. We have our lives, but when we are done we go back to the earth and new life begins. Death is a part of life."

The probable death of the irises becomes part of my life just as Kelly's and Gus's deaths had two decades earlier, teaching me that a book's advice is only as good as the compliance it receives—teaching me to open my eyes and ears to the world to see if the advice remains applicable. Teaching me patience.

Despite guilt over my wrongheadedness with the irises, I am beginning to see that death does not mean failure, either for those who die or for those who are left behind. Death is not a "bad" thing. In the garden some plants thrive and some plants struggle—there is no "good" or "bad" to this—merely fact. Working with plants every day, I see some respond to water while some continue to droop. Most are helped by fertilizer, but I've yellowed my share with too much of that good thing too. Some bloom as if they have so much to say they just can't say it all with the few stems available to them, and some hardly speak at all, maybe just a bud that never opens.

There is a horticultural explanation to all of this, I know. Genetics or a soil sample can probably tell the factual story, but each day in the garden, summer or winter, tells the personal story. The world is a garden of personalities, including those of plants. They, like people, do not live forever. I am not angry at them for dying (okay, maybe sometimes I wish that a four-dollar investment would have panned out a little better) and I try not to be angry at myself for not keeping them alive. Sometimes the last part is the hardest, even now.

I know that the irises I have so mindlessly destroyed will do their part to help create new life. Death is not the end for them, not really. Microbes are being fed. Soil is being enriched. Humans are learning things. The irises are leaving the world different from the way they found it. No matter what we do on this earth, when we leave it *is* different from the way we came into it whether we are iris, calf, or gardener. Everything we do changes something.

Did you ever wonder how to fertilize irises? The American Iris Society advises against using anything too high in nitrogen because it "encourages soft growth that is susceptible to disease." The best times to fertilize are in the early spring (before bloom) and about a month after bloom. Using weed/feed products is not good for the rhizomes, despite the fact that weeds love to seed themselves in between those bulb-like structures, where they are next to impossible to get out. Oh, yes, and the Iris Society advises that rhizomes should be planted at least four to six weeks before the first killing frost (which in Minnesota is usually around September 15 rather than December 15 as my futile planting effort indicated.) Better too early than too late is my advice . . .

# 22

# Foreigners

Despair over the Great Iris Fiasco eases as snow buries the garden and I no longer have to greet the proof of my stupidity every time I walk to the mailbox. As sub-zero temps begin to subside, I hope for an iris miracle, regularly checking magnolia branches and patches of grass for signs of spring. The first sign appears without my even noticing.

Owls move in on a winter's day when I am not watching. Hawks are not watching either, or they might not allow the nest they have worked so hard to build to be usurped by someone else. But hawks are not nesting yet. They are busy with what hawks do, that watching of the world through the jaded eyes of the under-employed. Owls have a different schedule.

I have noticed the nest at different times when I was sitting in the car with the engine idling, waiting for the garage door to open. For months it was just a cluster of sticks high in a tree beyond our brush/habitat pile. A deep ravine slopes off to the north below the nest, giving it the instant elevation so beloved of pilots, human and otherwise. Deer trails crisscross the ravine, some of them traversing deadfall from last summer's storm that toppled sixty trees in our woodlot and windbreak—none on the house, for which we are thankful.

  The fallen trees all lie headed southeast, neatly parallel, along the outer edge of the woods, and we berate ourselves for not being able to cut them for firewood. At the same time we remind ourselves that, like the brush pile, they offer habitat for wildlife. They actually fit in with our Woodland Stewardship Plan. As they decay, they will offer habitat for microorganisms. We try not to think not of what we have lost, but of what we might gain.

  Fifty feet above the forest floor, the hawks' nest clings to a tall red oak in the middle of the woods. I am used to seeing it up there, three hundred feet behind the garage but on a line with the building's ridgepole. A large, dark spot yet immediately identifiable against the pale winter sky, it defines itself clearly compared to the mess of leaves stuffed in the crotch of two branches that makes up a squirrel's nest.

  This one is wider and flatter, made of sticks, and it balances midway out from the trunk on some small branches. I have grown so used to the configuration of the empty nest that the first time I see an owl in it I think surely it is something else. A squirrel? A chunk of bark fallen in and standing upright? I think I see ears. But that couldn't be—the nest is too far away for me to make out ears. I'm imagining something. Still, even to my unpracticed eyes, something is different about the nest. And something is definitely in it.

  Now I check it every time I walk onto the driveway. Sometimes the nest appears to be occupied, sometimes not. When the snow melts a little, I walk into the woods toward the nest for a better look, but the closer I get, the less I can see. The angle is all wrong. This nest can only be viewed from afar, just as nature, no doubt, intended. Only when, a few days later, I see a bird fly onto the nest do I identify it as a bird even most school children know. A great horned owl, complete with ear tufts, *is* in residence.

From the beginning, I know what owls in residence mean to the woods. They mean that other birds are at risk. They also mean rodents are at risk, although this somehow does not bother me the way the idea of birds at risk does. An owl in the nest tells even a country novice like me that young owls will soon follow, even though the weather remains cold and other birds are not yet nesting. More risk.

I watch the nest closely as February fades, always feeling that I, too, am being watched. Once, when I finally find a pair of binoculars, I see the owl's head turn when I walk from side to side. I seek out the *Sibley Guide to Bird Life and Behavior* and learn that owls are very serious about the business of nesting, that I should keep my distance or risk being attacked. Ah, so I am at risk, too.

Well, now the owl's nest takes on an even greater significance. I respect the ability of the owl to instill both fear and awe in me as I watch the buds swell on the big magnolia tree, knowing its white flowers may surprise me even before the snow is gone. I am waiting for the snowdrop bulbs I planted last fall to prove themselves as early as the catalogue said they would be. I wait, but snow still covers much of the ground and the woods are brown-gray with winter's dinginess, which I now see provides the perfect cover for nesting owls. *Mother Nature really has it all figured out.*

Sometimes, of course, even brown-gray trees can't help the owls. Crows find them and mob the nest, circling and cawing until the owl flies. Oddly, crows do not attack the nest, but instead chase the owl. When the owl tires of the game, he or she glides back to the nest, crows in tow, and just waits them out. The next day it all begins again.

The female owl, now sitting on the nest at all times, does not make a sound during the day when I am outdoors. The "whoo-whoo" so familiar at night is still until one day, as I stand looking up to the nest from the small clearing where we back up to our ever-increasing brush pile, and call "whoo-whoo, whoo-whoo". Without my binoculars I see the owl straighten up to twice the height usually seen above the rim of nest sticks. I see wings flutter just a little. The brush pile is between us, but still the wings ruffle just enough to make me wonder if I am at risk that moment. Just enough to make me wonder if it is wise for me to turn my back and walk toward the house.

I take the risk and turn away. Before I have moved more than a foot or two, I hear, "whoooo-who-whooo". Not the same call I made, but close enough to stop me and make me turn around. We have communicated, she in her house and I next to mine. Foreign sovereigns with no telephone lines, we call to each other across the abyss of trees just to hear the sound of one another's voice.

I think of the times I have met international travelers and have tried to greet them in their native tongue. I remember that their delight overrides their chagrin at my mispronunciation. I see that owls, too, are generous. They are as curious as I am. They are smart (even wise, as legend has it) and they do not attack people smart enough to keep their distance. Our conversation done, the owl and I resume our daily activities.

There are many owl calls in the evenings during this nesting time, and sometimes I call back. The more I try, the better my calling becomes, but I don't want to be too good. I remember the risk, and I remember hearing that Native American legends say that the owl's hoot foretells death. It is only after I begin to study owl lore that I learn just as many legends say that owl sightings portend pregnancy (Wales), or are related to lightning because they brighten the night (China), or help women find husbands (Alsace-Lorraine). Nevertheless, most of the legends link the owl to unsavory happenings, and nearly every culture has its own legend. In Scotland it was once believed to be bad luck to see an owl in the daytime. I check my life insurance policy.

Why do we assign spiritual significance to the owl when we don't most other birds (except for crows, ravens, peacocks and a handful of others)? Perhaps in ancient times the owl's upright stance and saucer-like eyes signaled something that we no longer understand. Maybe there is something that connects us with the owl and we acknowledge the connection even though we cannot prove it rationally, even though we set ourselves high above all other creatures and plants. Such a connection, if there is one, has worked in the owl's favor. It remains a protected species. Maybe other species would be safer if they appeared to have a spiritual dimension as well.

As the owls call at night, I honor their right to free speech just as they endure my shouting over snow blowers and car engines during the daylight hours. There is much we could speak about—were we both on the same nocturnal or diurnal schedule. Their ancestors were here first. We are interlopers. We, too, have moved into a house where the spirit of the former owners still lingers. We, too, have pushed our children from the nest, helped them fly, and encouraged them to go far from home so that they can have their own lives. We go on speaking about these things, but not to each other. There is too much risk.

I come to wonder about all that takes place at night while the owls hunt and nurture. Their feathers are specially designed for silent assault. They could be anywhere at any time, undetected. They are equipped with special tools like extra-sensitive triangulated hearing. Because they are so hulky and huge, without enhanced senses they could never surprise any prey. Instead, they are masters of deception.

The greatest threats to owls today are habitat devastation and pesticides. I am glad I didn't use much Round-Up last summer, and suddenly I wish I hadn't used any. I am also suddenly glad that we've procrastinated about burning our brush pile, because I know it houses many meals for the owl. At least we may be doing *something* right.

In early March I sense a difference in the rim of the nest and suspect that the babies have been born. I think I see some movement, but at first I am not sure if it is the mother hovering or the babies wiggling. In a few days I know: it is babies, wiggling—trying to peek over the nest's edge, trying to see the world below, probably begging their mother for a chance to get out on their own. She does not oblige.

For nearly a month the young owls remain, five in all, growing bigger until they almost overflow the nest. I do not see them climb out onto a branch a few weeks later—no doubt their parents make them do that at night. I do not know if any of the younger ones are eaten by the older ones, which I learn is often the case, but there seems to be an abundance of owlets in the nest whenever I look. I do not go close enough to find out if any have fallen out onto the ground. I give them space, yet I check the nest several times each day as I walk outdoors.

And then one morning they are all gone. Without ever giving me a glimpse of their soft young bodies, they disappear, dispersed to far-off places so as not to infringe upon their parents' domain, Sibley's book tells me. They can range off for up to ten miles. But many don't make it. They are killed on the road where they are hunting rats that have come to eat from the fast food boxes littering the highways. Some are killed by predators, although few are shot, because their territory is the night—not an easy time to hunt, unless one *is* an owl. Owl parents may separate for the year, perhaps coming together again in the next breeding season but perhaps not. They are likely, however, to stay in the same area and be monogamous.

This, to me, does not sound evil, dark, or otherworldly. I take it on observation that owls are just like any other species: they do what they need to do to survive. I only wish they were not so nomadic. I want to get to know them better, like the chickadees that land on my mitten in the winter. But owls do not exist to please me. They exist to make the world a richer and more beautiful place. They exist to fulfill their own needs and to be the fulfillment of other species' needs. They exist as living lessons in diversity. They exist because, so far, I have not screwed up the world so badly that they cannot exist. They exist to provide a mystery I cannot completely solve, which everyone knows is the best kind of mystery, the kind of mystery that keeps one turning pages far into the night where owls thrive.

The more I learn about owls, the more I am thankful I took a risk by imitating their call. Some would say I made a fool of myself, yet watching nature and not interacting with it on some level is like a teenager having a crush on a movie star. We, however, cannot afford not to interact because we cannot just move on to a crush on something else. A relationship with the earth, unlike a simple crush, I am learning from the woods and gardens, develops over a lifetime through interactions large and small, foolish and wise. My relationship with owls helps me to see that I fit into the owl's existence just as he fits into mine. We are partners in this woodland corporation.

Today as I cross the driveway, the snow is melting. I take a close look at the ravine that drops off on the north side and realize that it isn't eroding because wild grapes and red-twig dogwood and daylilies' fleshy roots are holding the shoulder slope intact. I am less pleased that quack mars this pleasant combination and I make a mental note to try to weed this area in early spring and make it look nicer.

I also note that our house is protected from the wind and sun by the same trees that housed the owls. Robins are already nesting by an eave spout, but owl nesting time has passed for another year. Still, I look up over the garage ridgepole as if an owl might be there doing a little spring cleaning, but of course it is not. I will have to be satisfied with hoping that next February owls may move in again when I am not watching.

Did you ever wonder why owls have such large eyes? Actually, their eyes, though large, appear larger than they are because around them are tiny feathers that make up what are called "facial disks." These facial disks help funnel sound to their ears, which are located close to the eyes. Some owls have ears placed asymmetrically in order to maximize their hearing for night hunting— so maybe they are glad we focus on their eyes as the hallmark of their beauty.

# 23

# A Moving
# Experience

By the time March comes around, I know that owls are still patrolling the woods. I am still patrolling the gardens for even the smallest sign of life. The long row of lifted and replanted yellow irises has none, but the quack is already beginning to assert itself. Not even *I* manage to kill everything.

On the west side of the house, a shady wild garden took care of itself all of last year while I worked at trying to grow vegetables, clean up weeds, and freshen roses. Like the big garden, where the four problem rows reside, this one is on a slope so that when people drive into the driveway, they look up and see wild phlox, American spikenard, ostrich ferns, and some non-native plants placed there by the previous owners.

At the of the garden top stands a lightweight metal arbor made of woven wire and hollow aluminum tubing, a structure also set in place before we arrived. Leaning toward the house as if it wished it could come inside, the arbor gives a quaint, old garden look to the relatively new (twenty-year-old) gardens and their ageless natural cousins, except that now, with the frost coming out of the ground in the same sinking-rising action that causes potholes, the poor arbor is not just leaning—it's ready to topple over.

When I check the clematis I have planted on one side, the sight of last year's spindly, sun-starved vine wakes me up to the fact that straightening up the arbor will not be enough to help the clematis be the plant it should be. The *jackmani* needs to be moved, and the arbor with it. The *virginianna* on the other side of the bent-over contraption needs a new home, too.

If the ground isn't too frozen, which I hope desperately it isn't, I decide this is the day that I am going to move the arbor to flatter ground. I have a dream of seeing it square at the corners instead of trapezoidal—a small thing, but then not all dreams have to be big. I also dream of the profusion of purple and white blooms that I have seen on other people's clematises.

Contemplating the whole task fills me with a certain amount of trepidation. One garden book I consult advises against moving clematis—ever. I know better than to say I have nothing to lose, because I have, quite literally, two clematises to lose, but last year's lack of performance tells me they will languish again this year if I don't get them out from under the canopy of pin oaks and box elders that conspire

to make sure that they will never bloom. I have a shot at giving them a better life if I move them, and moving them while they are totally dormant seems like the logical approach.

The green garden tractor and red trailer make their first appearance of the year, and I feel like I am getting re-acquainted with two old friends. Because I seem to be mentally incapable of backing up with a trailer, I unhook it and push it next to the arbor, then back the tractor up to it, and rehook it. I am thankful it is only a small trailer and that the ground is firm enough that I don't leave ruts. I am also thankful to be able to get in close with it, because I suspect that the clematis clumps will be heavy.

The arbor itself, weighing less than ten pounds, is anchored by two pieces of—what else?—rebar, each of them about eighteen inches long. They are wired to the wire mesh, which is attached to the hollow metal arbor frame. Wire! All wire! Nothing solid! No wonder this arbor fell over. I lift it easily onto the trailer and then dig up the clematises on either side, placing them and their many pounds of attending soil in the trailer. Next, I proceed very, very slowly toward the perennial garden.

The perfect site for the arbor waits, between the ends of the long peony row and the long daylily row, which right now, in the early spring, are just beginning to put up a little new growth. I have often silently criticized arbors stuck willy-nilly in the middle of lawns where they are not part of a path and do not have plants growing on them. They seem to exist solely because people like the *idea* of an arbor, but don't really know what it is for. Now *I* am about to install my arbor in a spot where it will be, by far, the tallest and loneliest thing around unless lots of volunteer sunflowers outdo themselves this year. If the clematises don't bloom out here in the garden, my arbor is going to look just like the ones I have long disparaged. Pride goeth before a fall.

Having discarded the obviously too-short rebar pieces that had supported the arbor previously, I pound in two lightweight fence posts with winged bottoms, then thread them through the woven wire on the arbor, pounding them down further once I have set the arbor in its new home. I walk back to the previous site, get the rebar, and pound it in on the opposite corner from the fence posts for good measure. The arbor still leans a little. At least it leans in full sun, and the corners are (almost) square. Some dreams do come true.

The soil is still soaking up the snowmelt, and so I am unable to work the soil before I set the clematis in. I dig holes only slightly larger than the root balls and disturb them as little as possible. The *jackmani*, which I had brought along from our previous home, seems especially precarious. I have already moved it once more than the law allows, and here I am moving it again because it has never bloomed in its entire seven-year life anyway, only vined its way half-heartedly through each of them.

Now I wonder if attention may make it bloom at last. I admit, however, that it and *virginianna* may quite possibly have been killed by my moving them, joining the hundreds of possibly dead irises on what is turning out to be my garden death march. But, still, there is hope because it is spring, when all things are possible.

This whole operation has taken less than four hours, and when I stand back to admire my handiwork, I am struck by how the vertical lines of the arbor—even now while it is bare—add a new dimension to the garden. I have been so focused on the existing perennials—and the quack—that I haven't given much thought to what books call the "bones" of the garden. Now I see that I've just added a vertebra (or maybe it's an arm). I quickly look around to see what else might be in want of transplanting, what one of my fellow gardeners calls "rearranging the furniture."

Most of the plants that seem to be in the wrong place are short in stature: the irises I brought from the other house are errantly planted in the white garden (oops). Some rose bushes near the house have come to be in full shade (though I know they were probably in full sun when they were planted). The woods are determined to fill in the open space around the house, bending their lovely branches ever closer, and I am beginning to see that our job is not just to care for the woodlot, but also to keep it at bay so that we can care for our house. For now, three miniature roses, still in their dormant state, are dispatched to join their sisters in the rose garden where they fill in some empty gaps that were hitherto heckled by thistles and their ilk. More flowers and fewer weeds? Talk about a win-win situation.

Being one of those people who moves her living room furniture around every few months, I enjoy this business of transplanting things in the garden. After going through the height, color, sun needs, and soil conditions considerations for a plant, I don't hesitate to move it to a new site if that seems a better fit. Using Judith Handelsman's advice to speak to each plant as it is moved comes naturally to me, I realize, as if I am speaking to children.

An impetuous transplanter, however, I do not seem to be able to adopt Handelsman's advice about asking the plant where it would like to be planted twenty-four hours in advance of moving it. I make a mental note to plan ahead better in the future so that I can test out Handelsman's advice in a more scientific manner.

Nevertheless, a few days later the clematises signal me that they like the new place. Healthy, leafy shoots have burst out of the ground next to the leaning arbor like—dare I say it?—quack. They wander aimlessly on the ground until I help the first one find its way to the diamond-shaped wire mesh on the arbor. After that, my help is not needed, or probably appreciated. These, obviously, are plants with a mission, with pent-up desires that can no longer be denied.

With each transplant, I realize I am creating for that organism an event as cataclysmic as a move to a different city or state would be for me. The plant will have new neighbors who may or may not make it welcome. It will have to adjust to more or less wind, more or less runoff when rains come, perhaps even a slightly richer or poorer soil. It may find itself in the path of browsing deer or rabbits. I am trying to help the transplant be upwardly mobile, but that in itself can be a stressful path. Humans know that from their own life journeys. Plants are no different. I speak in soft tones, humbled.

Comedians make jokes about people like me who talk to plants. I don't mind. They allow that maybe plant talk is okay as long as you don't think the plants are answering you back. Any gardener knows, however, that plants *do* answer you back, just not in English. The two clematises, happily making their way up the sunlit arbor, are sending me a message: "Thanks." The roses that bore no blooms in last summer's woodland shade were sending me an S.O.S. The garden itself, looking spiffy with the addition of its new/old arbor seems to be saying, "At last!"

Every living organism, I'm convinced, has a language. Brule, with her expressive spaniel eyes, her thumbs up/thumbs down tail messages, and her ever-active nose certainly has hers. Humans, in their arrogance, assume that language must be verbal, even written down. Plants have written their histories across the ages, and we are continuing to learn how to read them. As we lose species to global warming and pollution, we are reminded that we need to take plant languages more seriously. Many people think reading plant messages is only important if the plant is useful to humans for medicine, food, or anthropological research. Yet every organism is useful to the world somehow. Except quack, I'm sure.

With the coming of spring, I am once again plagued with doubts about my ability to eradicate quack from the garden because the snow is barely off the ground, and quack is already green. (I now know the meaning of the term "true perennial.") I have longed for spring as I waited through a long, snowy winter, and now it is here. With it, quack. If all living organisms have a language and a purpose, I tell myself, so must quack. Nevertheless, this year, I promise, I am going to get rid of it.

As a first step, I read all I can about it so I can use my time and muscles wisely. The University of Minnesota website gives me a bit of gripping news: yes, quack grass *does* have a Latin name. *Agrophron repens.* It's even hard to say. No wonder it's hard to kill. A friend tells me that the Latin name means "a sudden field of fire." I immediately relate to the wisdom of the definition.

Quack grass, I am delighted to find, was brought to us from England by our founding fathers and mothers. Mea Allan, in her book, *Weeds,* tells us that couch grass, as quack was called back then, came over with the Pilgrims. She says that by 1672, when John Josselyn wrote his book *New England's Rarities Discovered,* couch grass, quack, was already common here, along with other plants the immigrants introduced: shepherd's purse, dandelion, groundsel, sow thistle, stinging nettle, mallows, wormwood, chickweed, mullein, knot grass, comfrey, and plantain which, "Josselyn noted, the Indians called *Englishman's Foot*, as though it were produced by their very treading."

Plantain, I have come to realize, is the scourge of my shade garden areas. Second only to quack in my mind's eye. All from England, home of Sherwood Forest. Can any of this make sense?

Allan advises that *Agrophron repens* is "noxious and persistent…[and] sooner or later every gardener meets the abundant and far-creeping white or yellowish rhizomes winding their way through the soil, under and over and through the roots of treasured plants, and seemingly endless." Was my neighbor, who said she didn't have any quack in her garden lying? I doubt it. I make a mental note to ask her the secret, because I know that Round-Up can't be it.

Spring brings the raspberry issue to my attention again. From under the arbor, I can look directly across to the tangled briars that pass for our raspberry patch. Deer have browsed there all winter, and Brule's persistent hunting indicates scent of birds and rodents. Restoring the patch to some kind of order seems to be a necessary evil, for clearly it teems with life. Hiring a young neighbor to help with it seems the only solution. I make a mental note to call him as soon as I get back to the house. But, first I need to dig compost in around the rhubarb and the asparagus, I need to rake the deep mulch off perennials I've been neglecting, I need to haul out the hoses and the deck furniture, and the pots, and the cold frame I should already have been using for a few weeks, and on, and on. Winter is truly gone. Spring has come at last, except for the yellow irises.

Did you ever wonder about the difference between an arbor and a pergola? Both are intended to provide a spot of shade in the garden by letting vines climb up a wooden or metal structure. In short, they give the same effect that a large tree might, but at the same time they don't cause the competition for water that a shade tree would. Pergolas today are usually thought of as larger structures than arbors, a means of adding height and style to a garden—definitely not something I could move in my wheelbarrow.

# 24
# Walking
# Brule

There is an old saying in the Midwest that if you don't like the weather, just wait fifteen minutes. The day after the clematises signal me their happiness by the newly-sited arbor on that warm spring day, I wake up to four inches of light, fluffy snow. The good thing about spring snow is that I know it won't last more than a day or two, and often it provides much-needed soil moisture. If there is enough of it, it usually gives kids a day off from school and gives every activity the air of an unofficial holiday.

Today's snow isn't heavy enough to cause schools to close, but it has coated everything from the ground up in crystalline white. It is a snow so beautiful that even winter-weary Mid-Westerners gasp in awe and wish that the world could always sparkle with this kind of fairy tale beauty.

Brule is already thumping her tail against the wall, eager to get out into it, while I'm still savoring my coffee. Once out the door, summer or winter, the two of us have a regular routine. She sniffs the driveway. I sweep off the doorstep. She runs off into the woods. I start down the path to the bird feeders on the other side of the house. By the time I get to them, she is sitting at attention, waiting for me to empty an ice cream pail of sunflower and safflower seeds into the cedar tray. Her nose senses the birds that watch from every branch. The black-capped chickadee is always first to come and in deep winter will take seeds directly from my mittened hand. Today is different, as if the birds, too, know this snow is just a passing change.

Brule runs off to flush birds out of the nearby Scotch pine grove. Cardinals and blue jays and juncos fly out in all directions like water from a fountain. I scuff my Mukluks along in the new whiteness and wait for her. Every fluffy snowflake seems to sparkle independently in the eight o'clock sun. Brule's nose, deep in scent heaven, leaves narrow tunnels braided in the snow.

Finally, I walk back into the garage to wait a little longer while Brule trails an aroma near the edge of the woods. I don't bother to turn on the light because I know she will come running in in just a minute or two. When I turn back toward the open door to look for her, I am almost blinded by the brightness of the sugar-coated world against the dark-shadowed doorway. It strikes me as the reverse of those vision tricks where if you look at a bunch of small black marks on a white background long enough you will see a cow or Abraham Lincoln's face instead of just a bunch of black marks. This time, the doorway is like the frame around an all-white painting that has been dusted with diamonds. No branch or twig or weed has been left untouched. I step from the dark garage into a world of light, into the woods, into the painting.

I am only halfway across the driveway before I see a bird's wings perfectly imprinted on the fluffy crystals. So close to me, yet unseen. Whether this marks a take-off or a landing I'm not ornithologist enough to know, but I know immediately I want to see more, to know more. If I had not been here before the snow melted, as it surely will (and quickly under this bright sun), I would not have known the bird had been there. Yes, my life would have gone on and so, presumably, would the bird's, yet this imprint sends me an important message, for it lets me see how our paths with other living things cross in ways we cannot know.

I had sensed this interaction at other times as I worked with plants in the garden, or walked on deer trails in the woods, but I had been busy and set it aside. Now here it is, written down for me in the snow. I feel like I am reading a story I must finish before the clock runs out. Is this print the story of a bird's joy in finding some food on the snow, or of its struggle against a predator? I can't tell. All I can see is the perfection of the image, every feather tip distinctly outlined, the shape aerodynamically designed, the curves unbroken and pleasing to the eye. Looking at the print, I connect to a creature I cannot see or name. I sense it on a deep emotional level that makes me blink and hold my breath as if I, too, am suspended unseen in that cold air. In that moment, I am different—lighter than air, energy-filled, and in a state that must be something akin to bliss.

As if I have magic binoculars, I see details of the day everywhere. A leaf has drifted down from the burr oak just at the edge of the woods and even its meager weight has made an impression. When I lift it, its mark is still there, complete down to the veins in each lobe. My Mukluks are leaving their marks, too. What message does the squirrel take from those footprints? Or the cardinal? Or, for that matter, the oak?

I walk on, snow floating out from under each footfall like a Sunday football slow-motion shot, and suddenly messages seem to be whispering to me from every direction. It is all right there in front of me, and behind, and beside—and always has been. I have not been paying attention. Unlike Brule, who runs nose to the ground to read messages of scent only a spaniel can appreciate, I have not used my senses well. What is different about today? Why this day? Why these messages? Why me? Perhaps on this day something needs me to write them down? I run to the house for a clipboard, pencil and paper, and gloves to replace my heavy felted mittens.

When I get back, newly equipped to walk again under the knobby oaks and black cherry trees, I scurry like a squirrel to write down the messages I have already heard, as if I'm afraid they'll disappear. I have written a dozen or more before I realize, again, that they always have been there but I have not seen them. I scratch down message after message anyway, as fast as I can, my letters wild and backhanded.

With lines scrawled across the pages and my fingers getting cold in the thin gloves, I start back to the house again. I do not want to go in, but Brule is cold. The fresh snow has caked between the pads of her feet, and she wants it out of there. Pronto. I hurry in with her, then rush back out—with a camera this time (I who have never taken a decent picture in my life).

By the time I go back outside, not more than five minutes later, the sky has changed from sunny and blue to sunless and gray. The doorway doesn't frame the same kind of otherworldly painting now that it did just a half-hour earlier. I realize with a start that maybe the messages will *not* always be there in the same way.

Doorways open and we need to walk through them before they close. Maybe we risk never having them open again, I think, but then I discard the idea. Doors, by definition, are things that open. It is we who make the choice to walk through or not.

And so, I snap pictures of things that speak to me in the woods, and I feel an excitement unlike any I have ever experienced. As I begin, I'm certain the photos will be the best I have ever taken. I can almost see them framed and on our walls—inside and outside meet. Even though I am trying to be quick to retrace my steps so that I can photograph the same tree forms and vistas that sent me the messages I wrote on the clipboard, the snow is already beginning to melt and in many places bare ground reveals not only deadfall and brown leaves, but also moss and tufts of greenish grass I know have to be quack, or else quack's first cousin.

Can I, who have been waiting all winter for the world of green to come again, love green moss but still hate green quack? Kermit the Frog had it right: "It isn't easy being green". Just ask the still-brown irises.

I lower the camera and take a broader look. The saucer-size tufts of dull-green grass appear in open places throughout the woods, happily coexisting with the mattresses of moss. And they look beautiful there. I take a second look, and a third, to make sure they are not something else, but no, they are quack. Just quack. Just living its life as I am living mine. I can't help but speak to it: "Okay. Maybe I've been wrong about you. Sorry". As I turn my back on the rapidly melting snow, even I cannot believe that I have said a kind word to quack, yet I have. That is what is different about today.

What is also different about today is that I realize I have thought of the woods as separate from the garden—and I have thought of myself as separate from all of it. As Wendell Berry says:

> Perhaps the fundamental damage of the specialist system [of farming]—the damage from which all other damages issue—has been the isolation of the body . . . [so that] we find it easier than ever to prefer our own bodies to the bodies of other creatures and to abuse, exploit, and otherwise hold in contempt those other bodies for the greater good or comfort of our own.

Today I see that everything is a garden, some wild, some not-so-wild. Today I see that it is my habitat, my brush pile. Today I am not afraid of it. In fact, in this moment I feel totally at peace.

The Woodland Stewardship Plan, for all of its good intentions, just could not explain the concept of wholeness to me: I had to see it for myself. Now that I have, I wonder: Are the Siberian elms really weeds? Is any tree? How do we balance what is needed with what is invasive with what we like or want? Only by seeing woodlands, gardens, people, animals, soil, microscopic organisms, and all the rest as a whole can we begin to understand how holding back some species may help them, but may also harm others, and how total eradication is totally unhealthy but also totally possible.

Harrison B. "Bud" Tordoff, in the Foreword to *Minnesota's Endangered Flora and Fauna*, states that "our human spirit springs from a reverence for life, and a commitment to the preservation of species diversity is fundamental to an optimistic view of the future of our own species . . . we can do the most good for the greatest number of species by preserving functioning natural ecosystems wherever possible". In the woods this day, I see the ecosystem not at arm's length but as if I am one of its arms (or a hair on its head). When I go back inside, I read what I have scrawled on my clipboard:

*I came into the world one day*
*When I stepped outside my door.*

*I saw that even a short doorway will let a tall person pass*
*If the person is willing to bend.*

*I saw the trees say "Y"*
　　　　　*and "O"*
　　　　　　*and "U"*
*And I knew the world was talking to ME.*

*I saw that I am small sometimes,*
*And sometimes large.*
*Sometimes there are hurdles along the way.*
*If they are too high*
*I may need to make a new path,*
*Yet sometimes I am surprised at how high I can jump.*

*Face to face with the earth I saw*
*Ten thousand fronds on a clump of moss*
*Intricate grain in the wood of a fallen twig.*
*It is good to take a closer look.*

*Up close, I saw beauty in repetition;*
*Beauty in the unexpected.*

*We are all looking for something.*
*My dead tree stump is someone else's home, or supper.*
*Everything has a purpose.*

*In the tracks of fox and squirrel,*
*Deer and possum,*
*Cardinal, jay and crow*
*I saw that our lives cross in ways we cannot know.*

*When I came into the world I saw that even scars are beautiful.*
*I saw that dead trees still give life.*

*When I stopped, the clouds kept moving.*
*Above the tops of ancient oaks,*
*That is my world, too.*

*When I came into the world I saw that*
*Yesterday was still here today.*

*I saw that the best way to a destination is not always*
*A straight line.*

*I saw that even among others,*
*Some stand alone.*
*Some stand together.*
*There is no right or wrong way to stand.*

*When I came into the world I saw that there are paths*
*Through the thickest wood*
*If I just look for them.*

*I saw that the world is all around me*
*Not just ahead*
*Or behind.*
*I saw that there are worlds beyond my own.*

*I saw that I could never see it all,*
*But I did not give up.*

*No. I just closed my eyes*
*And let the world come into me.*

Every day there are messages. Some we decode and some we don't: the snow untouched and the snow as a blank sheet upon which all creatures write their stories of everyday living. I see that stories are also written when there is no snow and no one to read them. I see that there are so many kinds of beauty. I see that it is all there if I am open to connecting with it. If I am not, the world may just hit me over the head with its majesty anyway until I see it. This, I believe, is a miracle.

A few days later, when my photos arrive in the mail, I realize that my photo skills are as limited as ever. The photos are a dull, gray-brown and do not begin to show what I saw out in the woods that day. I can blame it on the disappearing sun, or on my inability to hold the camera still, or the wrong shutter speed, but the fact is that the dingy photographs send a message too and I take it with me: we can know the world, but we cannot capture it. If we don't like it now, maybe we just need to wait a few minutes and then open a door. I advise taking your dog too, if you are lucky enough to have one like Brule.

Did you ever think of keeping a botanical inventory of your garden or woodlot? You might be surprised to see how long the list is of plants you take for granted every day, which might inspire you to want to learn more about them and other plants you encounter. We may not be able to capture the world, but we owe it to ourselves and to the earth to learn more about how the whole thing works. Taking pictures is a wonderful way to track changes in plants, and to record plants that may disappear after an especially cold winter, or as the result of animal activity, drought, construction, and such. Even poor quality photos, as mine were, can provide many interesting clues about the plants around you. Whether you think of yourself as a botanist or photographer or not, you will find the time spent in making your inventory time well spent.

# 25

# Galaxy of Grass

After that snowy morning epiphany, I would like to say that I changed overnight. That I went from a wild-turkey-fearing wimp to a turkey-hugging fanatic. That I lost my fear of death and couldn't wait for my rose bushes to breathe their last, or for that matter for me to breathe my last; that I ceased holding out even the tiniest hope that quack might be eradicated in my gardens. That I followed up on all of those wonderful mental notes I made. But I didn't.

As April days drift by on strong breezes and cool rains, the perennials are slow to start. I am gripped with the fear that the gardens will not be as nice as they were last year, and that nothing will have lived through the winter.

I continue to uncover things as the weather warms, and find the hibiscus dead as the proverbial doornail under my artistic little mountain of mulch, brown right down to the soil line. I clear away the chopped leaves to let the ground warm up, holding out hope that later in the summer the plate-sized, pink flowers will slow down traffic out on the road when drivers try to figure out what that amazing plant is, but the possibility looks grim.

On the other hand, there are miracles. Iris miracles. All three rows of them withstood my impetuous autumn digging. Irises, it seems, can tolerate a lot of cold and are quite happy to sit on top of the ground all winter, still taking root in spring and blooming! Who knew? I don't, however, recommend the practice, especially for expensive hybrids, which might decide to revert to being plain yellow or purple irises instead of showy pink or blue-ruffled models.

Now I realize that I gave myself way too much credit for the amount of control I exerted over iris lives. Like the woods, they, too, do very well without me. Do they still have quack in them? Of course, but not nearly as much. I can coexist with it, and besides now I have a secret weapon: I know that I will lift them again every three years, and each time I do, it will improve the soil and discourage the quack. I realize that I owe the irises a debt of gratitude that I can never repay. Through their determination to bloom despite obstacles, and their willingness to work with me despite my many mistakes, they opened the door that let me read all the messages in the woods just a month ago in the snow. Now they are promising not just spring, but also summer.

June fifth brings on the full show of the miracle yellow irises, along with the burgundy, pink, and white peonies. Stately purple Siberian irises claim their due as well, all of them backed up by roses, with the single roses leading off. Most of these are somewhat de-quacked and seemingly very happy. The hibiscus doesn't even bother to watch. I wait. I scratch up the soil around last year's stalk. No new shoots. And still I wait. I feel failure heavy on my shoulders as I pull weeds and plant annuals. My $11.99 is probably gone, and I tell myself that the hibiscus was good while it lasted—still money well spent.

Near the end of June, the hibiscus finally wakes up. I decide that it must now be as warm in Minnesota as it is in Hawaii in January, and I sense that I would like Hawaii quite a bit. In any case, the mysterious clock that ticks only for plants sounds its alarm. Inside of three weeks, the hibiscus is three feet tall again and setting buds, blooming by the next week. I take more pictures. I have my husband take even more pictures, in case mine don't turn out. I make a mental note to save on prints by just having him take all of the pictures from this time forward. I will spend the extra cash on another hibiscus.

The huge pink flowers command attention in the garden again this summer. Yet as summer goes by I am just as attentive to my search for baby hostas in the grass. I look every time I mow the grass and every time I walk out to the garden. When I get down on my knees, I finally see them. I continue to learn to take a closer look.

When I check out last year's baby hostas, I find that one of them looks as though someone has stirred cream into two of its green leaves—the cross of two genetic lines has produced a new strain. Plant purists will gasp at the idea of propagating a cur such as this, but I see only its wonder. I love it for its differentness, for its assertiveness in the face of symmetry, for its proof of the constancy of change. This little cream-splashed hosta is the plant I'm happiest about having saved and, though I go through a short period of "too precious to plant" paralysis, I finally know that I have just the place for it—a prominent spot near the front door. I realize that I should give it a name too, but the very idea of that seems too big for me, just the way naming my own children once did.

Paul Gruchow's essay "Naming What We Love" from the book *Grass Roots: The Universe of Home,* helps me as I consider this:

> There are some whole living systems on earth—the soil ecosystems, for example, upon which we are utterly dependent for our sustenance—that remain almost as hidden to us as the galaxies beyond our own. Perhaps ninety-five percent of the organisms living in the soils have yet to be identified.
>
> It is true that we have named more of the earth's living things now than ever before, which would seem to be making headway. At the same time, under our influence the earth is experiencing its greatest rate of species extinction in at least tens of millions of years, and the rate has the potential to reach unprecedented proportions. Our net effect, then, is one of destroying, and thereby rendering forever nameless, more information about life on earth than we are gaining.

Gruchow goes on to ask if we can imagine being in a love relationship with someone whose name we do not know. In the years since his book went to press,

Internet dating has made such a situation not only possible, but actually quite acceptable and even wise. Still, as Gruchow says, "It is perhaps the quintessentially human characteristic that we cannot know or love what we have not named. Names are passwords to our hearts, and it is there, in the end, that we will find the room for a whole world."

Always one for alliteration, I consider that the hosta might be named Hope. Then I reconsider, out of respect to plant purists. How about Faith? After all, didn't I believe in it enough to save it from a life under the lawn mower blades? Or maybe Charity, because it gives me so much? I return to Hope, a name that embodies what I want for this plant: I hope that it will grow and prosper. I hope it will always remember both its humble and exalted place in the endless line of other organisms. I hope it will be able to put up with my care. It joins hosta *sieboldiana* and hosta *plantaginea* (and hostas I know only by their common names, like Drinking Gourd or Guacamole) in the little hosta world I am able to see and share.

It is on a spring morning a couple of years after Brule and I made our wonderful discoveries on the snow that I open the *Minneapolis Star-Tribune*, which is running the following headline (not on page one, mind you, but on page four) in letters about a half-inch high: "SCIENTISTS SAY THEY'VE GLIMPSED FARTHEST GALAXY."

Dateline: Paris. Astronomers in France have picked up light from Abell 1835 IR1916, 13.23 billion light-years away from Earth. Our universe is believed to have been born about 13.7 billion years ago, so this galaxy would have been formed when the universe was a baby. The new galaxy is in the Virgo constellation and is one-tenth the size of ours—but it's out there.

What else is out there at 13.5 billion light-years, and 13.6, and 13.7—and most of all, 13.8? What is beyond the beyond? Is there a neat edge to it all, the kind I wish I could manage to have on my gardens? Or are we in some kind of a cosmic box? Are we suspended in a vast nothingness wherein another Big Bang may someday create a whole new universe? Do we know what we know or do we have it all wrong? We may not know any of these answers, but we must not quit asking the questions just because the world beyond our world seems so obscure.

And so today, while I read about distant galaxies, I write about my own. I keep trying to unravel the infinite mystery in a blade of quack, which is just beginning to green. I recognize that even on my own acreage, I will never see it all, not *every* blade. Quack continues to baffle me, but also amazes me. I would be lying if I said that I love seeing it pop up in the garden, as it still does, but I can truthfully say that I finally understand what it is doing there (it doesn't know that this is my garden), and what is needed for us to peacefully coexist (better soil and a sharp hoe). However, I also see what Willa Cather once saw on her beloved prairie and described in her novel, *My Ántonia*: "As I looked about me, I felt the grass was the country, as the water is the sea…and there was so much motion in it, the whole country seemed, somehow, to be running."

Like Cather's country, mine seems to keep on running. I have walked our perimeter a few times, checked the fence and the survey markers and tried to figure out if the tree we were planning to cut was on our land or the neighbor's. I have wandered in the woods, mentally cataloging the trees, the wildflowers, the ferns, the kinds of brush that spring up in no apparent pattern. I have looked at rotted logs and stumps and praised their right to be just as they are. But I haven't seen everything. It all keeps changing, moving, growing, dying, running.

I haven't peered beneath every fallen oak leaf to see what lives there, and I certainly haven't taken a microscope out to the woods with me, but I would like to; I haven't climbed to the top of the tallest oak, or even the shortest one, to see the scratches left behind by the red-tailed hawk when he landed or took off. I haven't found out which creature lives in the hollow tree stump. What comes and goes

145

during the day or night I cannot know, though I wish I could. But this life goes on in spite of me, not because of me, and I must continue to learn that. I must be content knowing that I cannot know it all and cannot see it all. Unknown galaxies of plants I will never see grow in my lawn and gardens, in our fields and woodland. Multiply that by the billions of acres around the world and there is so much that I cannot see, that I cannot even begin to imagine it all.

I have seen, unfortunately, a scatter of sticks and skeletons under the place where the owl's nest sat up in the big oak tree. At the sight of the destruction, which some research tells me was probably caused by a storm rather than by a predator, a sense of loss fell on me like a fine mist until I remembered that owls could come again, to usurp a new nest. So far, however, the owls haven't returned, except to visit.

Still, change comes, in spite of us, but not always as fast as the changes in Minnesota weather. The intertwining nature of the garden and woodland, the owls and the moles, the people and the brush pile, has instilled in me a deep sense of respect for the way our amazing world coexists peacefully with itself. Everything in nature finds a purpose and a place, even though settling in may take trial and error as it has for me.

On that snowy day in the woods, I did not see it all, but one thing I *did* see was that the grass growing in the woods, grass that looked like quack, did not look like a weed there. It was just one part of the whole I know as the woodland. It did not look like "a herbaceous plant not valued for use or beauty, growing wild and rank, and regarded as cumbering the ground or hindering the growth of superior vegetation," which is how the *Oxford English Dictionary* defines a weed. In the woods, quack and its cousins look just fine. They serve a purpose too. There are times when quack is the only thing I can find to step on so as not to get my shoes muddy. In times like those, I am thankful for quack.

So, what is a weed, after all? Weeds have been defined as everything from "a plant out of place" to a plant that has an "ability to thrive almost anywhere." They have been described as having "bio-chemical resistance" (oh, yeah) and as "interfering with man's utilization of land for a specific purpose." All this being true, and much more, I find that I agree most with L.H. Bailey who said, "Nature . . . knows no plants as weeds," or perhaps with the poet Ralph Waldo Emerson who said a weed is only a plant "whose virtues have not yet been discovered." Ah, yes, and don't we all have undiscovered virtues?

And, so, my battle with quack ends with neither a bang nor a whimper, because it was never really a battle at all. It was a waiting game, I waiting for the quack to tell *me* what to do and the quack waiting for me to tell *it* what to do. Its job is to grow; my job is to get it to grow in road ditches, hillside pastures, and woodlands where it can do what it is so good at doing, which is to help control erosion. Surely the Pilgrims didn't bring quack here to make messes of their gardens.

In fact, the Pilgrims imported my nemesis because at that time quack grass was grown primarily for its value as an herbal remedy. An herbal written in 1653, stated, "Although a gardener be of another opinion, yet a physician holds half an acre of [quack roots] to be worth five acres of carrots twice told over." The roots are still used in South China to make an herbal tonic tea. The seeds can be used as a cereal: very fibrous (no kidding), and a gray dye can be obtained from the roots. Is this why the Pilgrims wore gray clothing?

There are dozens of medicinal uses for quack listed on the Journey to Forever website, but the one that strikes closest to home is the listing that says: "Couch (quack) grass is the favorite herbal medicine of dogs and cats, which seek it out and eat large amounts of it. Also liked by cattle, sheep and horses." Haven't I seen Brule eat grass (okay, and then sometimes throw up) nearly every time she goes to the garden and finds some that is just sprouting (again)? A plant in the wrong place, or a plant whose virtues have not yet been discovered—by humans? Dogs, it seems, may actually seek out quack as a means of easing a gassy or upset stomach. I make a mental note to think kinder thoughts of quack in the future.

Jane Grimsbo, Jewett of the Minnesota Institute for Sustainable Agriculture at the University of Minnesota, even goes so far as to say:

> My favorite plant that most people consider a weed—even a noxious weed—is quack grass. It is an excellent forage for cattle … it's drought resistant, tillage-resistant and appreciates manure. Interestingly, it is also recognized as allelopathic based on experiments in which root extracts from quack grass were used to water other plants, which inhibited their growth.

*Aha!* Even though I am growing kinder toward quack, I feel a little twinge of satisfaction that it has a documented dark side—it harms things growing close to it (unless one is trying to grow it as a crop, in which case it probably has no known predators and could become a super crop).

The future, with many more people vying for fewer resources, may restore quack to the elevated place it held when John Winthrop and the others brought it here. I hope they are smiling that one more convert has become at peace with it (mostly).

Quack, I have come to accept, cannot be eradicated, at least by me (though that would make my garden look very nice indeed). If it does turn out to be the plant that saves the planet from starvation, I can provide enough roots to feed multitudes. For now, when I see it in my garden, I may be frustrated by it, and I may wish that it would just go off and live in the neighbor's pasture, but I give myself permission to have a less-than-ever-ready-for-photo-op garden, which allows me to encourage flowers and discourage weeds, but to allow peaceful coexistence as well.

I'm not advocating letting quack take over the garden. Not at all. Nobody wants an allelopath loose in the roses or anywhere else. But knowing its habits, and the fact that it lives in our lawn, and that we never spray our lawn for weeds, I accept the fact that its roots have been here longer than mine and are not going anywhere. I surrender to its superior endurance and learn to discourage it in the garden by improving the soil quality, so that I can more easily remove the long, white-toothed roots. I learn to take great satisfaction when I gently pull, pull, pull and come to the end of one without breaking it, which is what happens in well-composted soil teeming with beneficial organisms.

The neighbor who said she had no quack was not lying, because she was very conscientious about soil improvement, yet I have a sneaking suspicion that down deep, even in her beautiful gardens, quack roots were just waiting for her to go on vacation.

In the garden, I see the benefits from grouping things together by color, or by species, or by growing habits, but I still don't know what makes combinations work some times and not other times. I can guess, but I can never really know, and it is what I do not know that keeps me gardening. Knowing I will never know it all is what makes me want to go out there each day to discover more, but it is also the thing that makes me able to dream, to theorize, to experiment. That I can get much of anything to grow, much less bloom, becomes a wonderful accomplishment when placed up against all that might be.

I still pull quack. And dig it. Occasionally I even try Round-Up, though I am never thorough enough to follow up with the second application that always seems to be necessary, and so I end up disappointed by the whole process. Mostly, I pull

the quack. When I do, and I feel something break, I know I've left some root behind though I cannot see it. I know it will come back to plague me later, but I keep on going. I continue to garden with a built-in denial mechanism that allows me to go on to the next weed where—hope springs eternal—I can do better.

What I finally learned, looking back on the first two years here, was that the only quack in the garden was me. I was a charlatan, coming to the country, pretending my life was separate from, and superior to, every other life—especially quack. Plants and animals taught me my place which, oddly, doesn't feel like a put-down at all, but instead like having an equal place in the world's flora and fauna inventory. They taught me that life shouldn't stay the same, can't stay the same. Life changes with every breath we take, with every breath the cottonwood takes, or the raccoon. If we are looking for perfection, we will not find it in the perfect edges of a garden, but in all that surrounds it—sky and tree and wild turkey and, yes, even quack. We will not find it in trying to control everything we encounter.

Life in this new place has made me confront my fears: the fear that I couldn't take care of gardens, the fear that I would be frightened by wildlife, the fear of all that I didn't know—the fear of failure. Out of fear comes the realization that some limits are beneficial, like letting turkeys be turkeys and sunflowers be sunflowers, but not *always* letting buckthorn be buckthorn. Fear will not harm us as long as we do not allow it to be the final answer. In fact, fear sometimes saves us from ourselves, but it often requires a scapegoat. Mine was quack.

The world, our little corner of infinite galaxies, begs us for a closer look and teaches us that if we take it we will learn that there are no failures in live things, or even in dead ones. We are part of a whole beyond our wildest dreams. The only two things we need to fear are the failure to embrace the world's boundlessness and the failure to restore what is lost and recycle what is left.

I knew I was starting to fit into my new place when I began to communicate with that wild turkey. The true sense of place, however, runs much deeper and is born of both giving and accepting. It comes from walking beaches and from rubbing elbows with oaks, from savoring sweet raspberries and from the sublime scent of an old rose. The poet Kabir describes it well: "All know that the drop merges into the ocean but few know the ocean merges into the drop."

A simple drop of quack has taught me that the world is very much *not* about us and very much about a galaxy of other lives, all with their own story. The world is not a finished product we are enjoying, or enduring, for a time. It is a sea of change, a story we write ourselves into as we go along. A story that writes us.

# Appendix

**Woodland Stewardship Plan.** Minnesota Forestry Association, Carol Cartie, Administrative Assistant, 26874 County Road 411, P.O. Box 496, Grand Rapids, MN 55744 (218) 326-6486.

**Land Stewardship Project.** 821 East 35th Street Suite 200 Minneapolis, MN 55407 (612) 722-6377; Fax: (612) 722-6474.

**Writers Rising Up.** Writers Rising Up encourages a deeper understanding and participation in environmental stewardship. Through the literary arts at community events, contests, workshops, literary performances, interpretive installations and publications, our focus is on nature education and writing. We promote writers who associate their work to cultural, spiritual and social connections to place, the land, natural habitat, including flora, fauna and wetlands.

**Writers Rising Up.** 16526 W. 78th St., #163, Eden Prairie, MN 55346. Writers Rising Up is a 501(c) (3) public charity. Contributions are tax deductible.

**University of Minnesota Master Gardener Program Information:** Email us at: University of Minnesota Extension Master Gardener State Office, Department of Horticultural Science, 155 Alderman Hall, 1970 Folwell Avenue, St. Paul, MN 55108.

**University of Minnesota Extension/Garden:** UMN Landscape Arboretum Yard & Garden Desk Weekends 10:00 am - 4:00 p.m. UMN Landscape Arboretum Yard & Garden Line (952) 443-1426.

**University of Minnesota Minnesota Landscape Arboretum.** 952.443.1400. Mailing address: 3675 Arboretum Drive Chaska, MN 55318.

# Bibliography

Allan, Mea. *Weeds: The Unbidden Guests in Our Gardens.* Viking Press, New York, 1978.

Ausubel, Kenny. *Seeds of Change: The Living Treasure.* HarperSanFrancisco, 1994.

Berry, Wendell. *The Gift of Good Land: Further Essays Cultural and Agricultural.* North Point Press, San Francisco, 1981.

Berry, Wendell. *The Unsettling of America: Culture and Agriculture.* Sierra Club Books, San Francisco, 1977.

Brandenburg, Jim. *Chased by the Light.* Creative Publishing International, Second Edition, October, 2001.

Cather, Willa. *My Antonia.* Simon & Brown, November, 2011.

Coffin, Barbara, and Lee Pfannmuller, editors. *Minnesota's Endangered Flora and Fauna.* University of Minnesota Press for the Minnesota Department of Natural Resources, Minneapolis, 1988.

Culpeper, Nicholas. *A Modern Herbal*, London, 1653, as quoted in journeytoforever.org.

Dickinson, Emily. *Final Harvest: Emily Dickinson's Poems.* Selection and introduction by Thomas H. Johnson. Little, Brown & Co., Boston, 1961.

Friend, Catherine. *Hit By A Farm: How I Learned to Learned to Stop Worrying and Love the Barn.* Marlow and Company, New York, 2006.

Frost, Robert. *You Come Too: Favorite Poems for Young Readers.* Holt, Rinehart and Winston, New York, 1959.

Gray, Ed. *Track Pack: Animal Tracks in Full Life Size.* Illustrated by DeCourcy L. Taylor, Jr. Stackpole Books, Mechanicsburg, Pennsylvania, 2003.

Gruchow, Paul. *Grass Roots: The Universe of Home.* Milkweed Editions, Minneapolis, Minnesota, 1994.

Handelsman, Judith. *Growing Myself: A Spiritual Journey Through Gardening.* Plume, New York, 1997.

Hessayon, Dr. D.G. *The Rose Expert.* Expert Books, London, Third Edition 1993.

Leopold, Aldo. *A Sand County Almanac.* Ballantine Books, New York, 1990.

Luxton, George E. *Flower Growing in the North: A Month-by-Month Guide.* University of Minnesota Press, Minneapolis, 1956.

Minnesota Department of Natural Resources. *Woodland Stewardship Plan.* St. Paul, Minnesota, 1991.

Rustad, Orwin A. *A Journal of Natural Events in Southeastern Minnesota.* Riverbend Nature Center, Faribault, Minnesota, 1997.

Sibley, David Allen. *The Sibley Guide to Bird Life & Behavior.* Alfred A. Knopf, New York, 2001.

Snyder, Leon C. *Trees and Shrubs for Northern Gardens.* University of Minnesota Press, Minneapolis, 1980.

Steiner, Lynn M. *Landscaping with Native Plants of Minnesota.* Voyageur Press, Stillwater, Minnesota, 2005.

Thomas, Graham Stuart. *Shrub Roses of Today.* J.M.Dent & Sons, Ltd., London, 1985 reprint edition.

# Quoted Material

Chapter Two: Berry, Wendell. *The Unsettling of America*, p. 97. Frost, Robert. *You Come Too*, p. 64.

Chapter Seven: Gruchow, Paul. Grass Roots: *The Universe of Home*, p. 209.

Chapter Eleven: Kenny Ausubel, *Seeds of Change: The Living Treasure*, p. 21.

Chapter Sixteen: Thomas, *Shrub Roses of Today*, p. 32. Dickinson, Emily. *Final Harvest: Emily Dickinson's Poems*, p. 166.

Chapter Twenty-Three: Handelsman, Judith, *Growing Myself*, p. 19. Allan Mea. *Weeds: The Unbidden Guests in Our Garden*, p. 17and 98.

Chapter Twenty-Four: Berry, Wendell. *The Unsettling of America*, p. 104. Coffin, Barbara, and Pfannmuller, Lee, editors. *Minnesota's Endangered Flora and Fauna*, p. xi.

Chapter Twenty-Five: Gruchow, Paul, Grass Roots: *The Universe of Home*, pp. 126-26 and 130. Allan, Mea. *Weeds: The Unbidden Guests in Our Garden*, p. 12. Culpeper, Nicholas, *A Modern Herbal*, 1653. jouneytoforever.org/edu_quackgrass.htm.

# Acknowledgments

Thanks to Writers Rising Up to Defend Place-Natural Habitat-Wetlands, and especially to Vicki Price, for championing nature writing and for encouraging writers to redefine place in our changing world. To the Zumbrota *News-Record* for first publishing the essay "Foreigners," and to *Turtle River Press* for first publishing "Roses in the Snow," both of which are adapted in *Quack*, my thanks. Thanks, also, to Marie Marvin and Crossings at Carnegie for fostering poets and artists. My deep gratitude to Seal Dwyer and everyone at North Star Press for helping this *Quack* to grow, and for supporting Minnesota writers. Special thanks to Corinne Dwyer for her lovely illustrations.

I am grateful to the Readers of OZ book group, who first listened to the lines from "*When I Came Into the World*," and to everyone in OZ (Oronoco Presbyterian and Zumbrota UCC) whose open and affirming presence carried me along as I lived and wrote *Quack*. Thanks to Rev. Kitty Burbo for teaching me so much about dealing with all kinds of quack in life.

Catherine Friend dragged me kicking and screaming into a writing group. For this, I thank her, along with the other writing group members who were early readers of the manuscript: Maureen Fisher, Cindy Rogers, Selby Beeler, and Laurel Winter. I am grateful to poet Beverly Voldseth Allers for her encouragement, and also to Judy Wilder and Mary Sue Lovett who provided gardener's-eye reads of the manuscript. Thanks, also, to Marit Lomen for being my first reader and ever-en-courager, and to Joann Ronningen for sharing an appreciation of rural places.

Any success I've had in the garden or renovating the house owes much to Susan Quiring, whose enthusiasm and hands-on help were and are invaluable. Thanks to Ken and Dee Markson for continuing to grow this little corner of the world with us, and to Jim, Connie, and Billy Wendt for being our good neighbors, no matter where we go.

I am thankful to my three children writer children: To Sarah, for endless tech assistance, editorial advice and for sharing my garden passions. To Patrick, for giving me *The Writer's Book of Hope* and for letting me share in his writi ng process. To Steff, for her inspiring energy and for the example she sets in her writing.

Thank you, Bruce, for your endless support and willingness to go along with my many adventures. Sharing this place with you has been the experience of a lifetime.

To my flowers and woods, to Brule and Flag, thank you for teaching me so much. I love you all.